Jae –

Hope you enjoy –

Dori & Tom

I'll Be Home for Christmas

The Library of Congress
Revisits the Spirit of Christmas
During World War II

A Stonesong Press Book

DELACORTE PRESS

Published by
Delacorte Press
Random House, Inc.
1540 Broadway
New York, NY 10036

Sources and permissions are located on page 199, photo credits are on page
205, and constitute an extension of the copyright page.

Delacorte Press® is a registered trademark of Random House, Inc., and the
colophon is a trademark of Random House, Inc.
A Stonesong Press Book
Every effort has been made to preserve the integrity of the original texts.
All original punctuation and spelling have been maintained.

LIBRARY OF CONGRESS CATALOGING IN PUBLICATION DATA
I'll be home for Christmas : the Library of Congress revisits the spirit of
Christmas during World War II / [editor, Tom Spain, Michael Shohl].
p.   cm.
"A Stonesong Press book."
ISBN 0-385-33463-X
1. World War, 1939-1945—Personal narratives, American.   2. World War,
1939-1945—United States.   3. Christmas music.   I. Spain, Tom.   II.
Shohl, Michael.   III. Library of Congress.
D811.A21475   19999
940.54´8173—dc21   99-35252
CIP

Book design by Virginia Norey

Manufactured in the United States of America
Published simultaneously in Canada

October 1999

10   9   8   7   6   5   4   3   2   1

I'll Be Home
for Christmas

Contents

☆ ☆ ☆

The Stonesong Press would like to thank all those involved in the research, writing, design, and development of this book, including Athena Angelos, Gene Brown, Roger Bruns, Denny Downs, Ralph Eubanks, Laura Kreiss, Blaine Marshall, Sarah Scheffel, Michael Shohl, and Tom Spain.

Preface

☆ ☆ ☆

"WE MAKE WAR that we may live in peace," wrote the Greek philosopher Aristotle. Although Christmas is a season of peace, across five Christmas seasons many men and women served their country during World War II so that future generations could live in peace. In the pages of *I'll Be Home for Christmas* you will find an engaging collection of photographs and personal testaments from these men and women, all from a wide range of sources in the collections of the Library of Congress. Whether these stories are from the papers of General George Patton, a soldier's diary, or our recently acquired collection of memorabilia from entertainer Bob Hope, you will marvel at how the spirit of Christmas was kept alive during World War II both at war and on the home front.

The Library of Congress is pleased to join The Stonesong Press and Delacorte Press in publishing this unique perspective on the American experience during World War II. Preserving the American experience and making it accessible to all is one of the Library's primary missions. Although we are an institution whose collections are international in scope, we are most particularly the Nation's Library. Among the more than 115 million items in our collections are a wide range of materials covering the events of World War II. In fact, the Library of Congress is one of the few repositories in the world that can truly offer a full historical record from a variety of sources covering those six years of world upheaval.

The words and images in *I'll Be Home for Christmas* will stir as well as enlighten you. They may draw you to your own library or to the Library of Congress in Washington, D.C., or on the Internet (lcweb.loc.gov/exhibits) to find out more about the events of World War II you encounter here. Two of our on-line exhibitions: "Women Come to the Front: Journalists, Photographers, and Broadcasters During WWII" and "For European Recovery: The Fiftieth Anniversary of the Marshall Plan" will be of particular interest to those wishing to learn more about the Second World War. In the meantime, you have *I'll Be Home for Christmas.* It is an inspiring look at what has been called the largest single event in human history. Enjoy it, and happy reading.

James H. Billington
The Librarian of
Congress

I'll Be Home
for Christmas

I'll Be Home for Christmas

I'm dreaming tonight of a place I love
Even more than I usually do.
And although I know it's a long road back,
I promise you . . .

I'll be home for Christmas,
You can plan on me.
Please have snow and mistletoe
And presents on the tree.

Christmas Eve will find me
Where the love-light gleams.
I'll be home for Christmas,
If only in my dreams.

—KIM GANNON, WALTER KENT,
AND BUCK RAM

1943

Introduction

Christmas Memories of World War II

WAR AND CHRISTMAS—always they seem incongruous. In celebrating "Peace on Earth and Good Will to Men" amid the horror of organized slaughter, symbols and images clash. The carols and decorations, the gifts and religious ceremony, the trees and the parties—all of it, at wartime, plays against a backdrop of fear, against the reality of battle plans and bodies. And yet it is in these times that Christmas takes on a more urgent, immediate need. In these times, the complex human issues of mortality, of family, and of brotherhood are stark and real.

It was especially this way during World War II. Across the United States, the people coped. They shopped; they planned holiday gatherings; they sent cards. They shared the universal feelings of community and fellowship, of renewal and hope. But the tension was palpable, the nation stunned by death and destruction, by immense uncertainty and stories of horrors in far-removed places. Where, after all, were Corregidor and Bataan and Bastogne?

And on the battlefields, thousands of young men and women who had, only a few years past, yelped on Christmas mornings at the sight of new bicycles or BB guns or other kid things under the family trees now huddled in foxholes or worked at the front and faced unimaginable rigors and loneliness. Christmas meant home, warmth, security,

and a sense of roots; war was the antithesis of all of that. The young people had traded the bicycles for tanks or fighters or armored vehicles; the BB guns for .30-caliber machine guns and M-1 carbines; and the comfort for great peril.

No matter what the situation or the place, citizens and soldiers tried to recreate as best they could the feelings of Christmas. Medics decorated surgical tents with makeshift Christmas trees hung with water bottles and rubber gloves. Soldiers at the front lines gathered in bunkers for songs and prayers and joined in Communion in destroyed buildings. Most of all, they scurried to mail call for any word from home. Admiral William "Bull" Halsey once wrote to Admiral Chester Nimitz about cargo priority. "Please stop the flow of Washington experts and sightseers," he requested. "Each expert means two hundred less pounds of mail. I'll trade an expert for two hundred pounds of mail anytime."

During the war, each of the armed services sent photographers into the field. They took pictures, sent them back to the States, and wrote captions, some of them quite perceptive and moving. One of the hundreds of thousands of photographs sent back to Washington was of an Eighth Air Force airman kneeling in prayer in the sanctuary of an English church. The caption read: "He forgets his world for the moment . . . it is Christmas. It is Christmas, just like Christmas will always be . . . in his heart! Nothing can stop that. He offers his thanks that he has lived. He prays, as an airman prays, for courage and guidance—and for the safety and happiness of his loved ones at home. He prays for those he is fighting to set free . . . when Christmas morning comes again."

On the one hand, the war brought enormous stress and fear from dislocation and loss; on the other, it brought many together under one sustaining purpose—national survival. We see it in the letters, newspaper articles, sermons, journals, and music of the time and in the reminiscences of those looking back. Many seemed to stand stronger and more hopeful at Christmastime—the time of reunions, both real and imagined; of nostalgic and deeply personal stories and carols; of greater camaraderie and sense of belonging. This book is about those times.

1941

★ ★ ★

ON DECEMBER 7, 1941, at Pearl Harbor the world changed for America. For six years, in newspapers and on the radio and in flickering movie house newsreels, Americans had followed the seemingly inexorable drift toward world war. In October 1935 Mussolini's Italy invaded Ethiopia. Less than a year later, the Spanish Civil War erupted and from the pen of Ernest Hemingway came the warning that when the fascist bells tolled the death of a small country, the world was at risk. Indeed. In September 1939 Hitler's armies overran Poland. The Japanese soon moved again against their ancient enemy, China. France fell to Nazi armies in June 1941 and London fended off blitzkrieg.

The American government, still maintaining a desire for peace, helped the Allies with materials programs such as the Destroyers for Bases Agreement and the Lend-Lease Act. In an address asking for further aid to anti-Axis nations, President Franklin D. Roosevelt called for "Four Freedoms": freedom of speech and expression; the freedom of every person to worship God in his own way; freedom from want; and freedom from fear.

In August President Roosevelt and British Prime Minister Winston Churchill signed the Atlantic Charter on a warship in the western Atlantic, pledging themselves to the common goal of destroying Nazi tyranny. A month later missions from the United States and Britain met Soviet leaders in Moscow to pledge assistance in Russia's defense against Nazi aggression.

But life in the United States moved with seemingly few outward effects caused by these global concerns. In February Duke Ellington and his orchestra recorded one of the big band's all-time classics, "Take the A Train." In May the motion picture *Citizen Kane*, directed by and starring Orson Welles, premiered at the RKO Palace Theater in New York City. And in June a new cereal made its appearance on grocery shelves—O-shaped, ½-inch in diameter, .0025 ounce, it was first called Cheerie Oats.

On December 6 President Roosevelt sent a message to Japanese emperor Hirohito expressing hope that gathering war clouds would be dispelled. The following day, at 7:55 A.M. local time, Japanese warplanes attacked the home base of the U.S. Pacific fleet located at Pearl Harbor on the Hawaiian island of Oahu. Over four-fifths of the Pacific fleet was destroyed in less than three hours, eighteen ships sunk or seriously damaged, and about 350 planes destroyed or damaged. More than two thousand

A cartoon from Christmas 1940 that depicts Britain, personified as John Bull, asking Uncle Sam, as Santa Claus, for the passenger liner **Normandie,** *to help replace the severe shipping losses that Britain was experiencing from attacks by German U-boats and surface vessels.*

✫ ✫ ✫

Holiday trees are for sale at this Woonsocket, Rhode Island, gas station in 1940 for the last prewar Christmas. In hindsight, there is a certain innocence to this scene. In the first four decades of the twentieth century, the automobile had come to epitomize American society and culture, representing mobility, speed, and comfort. But in December 1941, this symbol of America would be largely mothballed. ★ ★ ★

Americans lost their lives. The next day the United States Congress declared war against Japan with only one dissenting vote.

Four days after Japan attacked Pearl Harbor, Germany and Italy declared war on the United States; the United States responded in kind. Within five weeks, the Japanese attacked Malaya, Thailand, Singapore, Hong Kong, Guam, Wake, Manila, and Corregidor.

On December 22 Prime Minister Churchill arrived in Washington, D.C., for a wartime conference with President Roosevelt. Christmas 1941 had come ominously.

A Fair and Moderately Cold Day in Beckley, West Virginia

In early December 1941 Jim Wood of Beckley, West Virginia, was sixteen years old. Forty years later he remembered those years and the front pages of his hometown newspaper carrying stories about Hitler's Germany. He also remembered something in those headlines about President Roosevelt dealing with the Japanese. But mostly he remembered the things with which teenagers were normally concerned—the movies, the local football champs, the radio, and a girl.

BECKLEY WAS NOT CONCERNED with war that Sunday morning. The big story of the day was the town's new $600,000 dial telephone system. That previous Saturday night, at exactly 11:59, Murell Ralsten, a descendant of Gen. Alfred Beckley, the city's founder, pushed a button switching Beckley from operator-processed calls to automatic dial telephones. A front page photograph showed Mayor A. K. Minter dialing the first number—9286—the home of Beckley Chamber of Commerce President E. G. Larrick.

Later that day, the Beckley Elks Lodge held its annual memorial service for deceased members. The speaker was Father John Halpin of St. Francis de Sales Catholic Church.

Shady Spring High School announced in the Sunday paper that a three-act comedy, "Aunt Minnie from Minneapolis," would be held the following day.

E. M. Payne Co. was holding a pre-Christmas sale on women's suede shoes—formerly $6.50 and $7.95 and reduced to $3.98 and $4.50. J. C. Penney was selling five-pound boxes of Christmas chocolates for $1 and one-pound boxes of chocolate-covered cherries for a quarter. Beckley Jewelry Store on Heber Street had seventeen-jewel Bulova watches for $24.75, United Dry Cleaners would clean and press men's suits for twenty-five cents, a new Electrolux sweeper was $49.50 and a twelve-ounce Pepsi was a nickel.

The undefeated and untied Mullens High School Rebels were the 1941 state football champs and the Stratton High School Bulldogs were the 1941 champions in Negro football. School desegregation was still years away.

At the Lyric Theatre, Bob Hope and Paulette Goddard were featured in "Nothing But The Truth," and at the Beckley Theatre Deanna Durbin, Charles Laughton and Robert Cummings were starring in "It Started With Eve."

There were fifteen shopping days until Christmas.

WJLS was the only radio station in town—today there are five—and every Sunday afternoon it carried the New York Philharmonic live from Carnegie Hall. The years have dimmed my memory of that concert but I think the featured work was Schubert's Eighth Symphony (The Unfinished).

Our radio was on during the concert but I was not listening. I was in the dining room with my mother, father and sister, having Sunday dinner. Our Boston bull terrier, Pug, sat patiently by, waiting for scraps.

Suddenly, one of my high school friends walked into the dining room and said, "The Japs have bombed Pearl Harbor." He kidded around a lot. Somebody chuckled. My mother invited him to get a plate and join us.

Come on into the living room, he said. It's on the radio. I went into the living room and the concert was being interrupted every few seconds by bulletins confirming the Japanese attack. There was a special announcement from Beckley American Legion Post thirty-two announcing an emergency meeting for later that evening.

Another friend arrived soon. He had a part time job at the radio station, so we accompanied him to the studio on Main Street where we spent an hour or so reading the news bulletins as they appeared on the UP [United Press] printer.

Later that afternoon the three of us walked down to Raleigh to visit another high school classmate—a girl. She was alone and we spent the rest of the afternoon just horsing around. I recall that at one point we took turns bouncing up and down on a bed. I don't know why. I guess it was because we were all very young and the war was still very unreal. We didn't talk about it much. Two years later, two of the three of us were in service along with most of the rest of the boys in the Woodrow Wilson High School class of '43. A few never came home.

As dusk fell, we made our way back to town and spotted a friend from Eccles who owned a car, a very popular fellow in those days because not many high school students had cars. He had parked on Heber Street in front of the Beckley Hardware Store. We got in and talked about the war and what branch of the service we would join.

Downtown merchants had put up a series of loudspeakers on Main, Heber and Neville streets for broadcasting Christmas carols, but that evening they had plugged them in to a WJLS line to carry the Pearl Harbor bulletins. President Roosevelt would address Congress the following day.

We listened to the war news and carols until about 9 o'clock, then separated and made our way home and to bed because Monday was another school day. We didn't know that December 7 had changed our world forever.

A Teenager in Hawaii

• Saturday, November 29, 1941

Got up planning to wash my hair, but it was so cold I talked myself out of it. Listened to the Army–Navy game while I printed Christmas cards. The navy won 14–6, darn it. We were leading 6–0 at the end of the first half, too. I finished forty-eight Christmas cards and I still have about thirty-six to go. Spent all afternoon doing nothing very exciting. Read the funnies when they came. Also read a few comic books and a little more of the "Berlin Diary." I wish I could finishthat. It's very interesting, but Mom wants to give it back to Colonel Lieutenant Went to show "Blondie In Society." Very funny!

• Sunday, November 30, 1941

Boy, is it cold!! Went to Weaver Beach. We were all wearing sweat shirts. Played volley ball, but didn't even get warm enough to perspire. I feel swell!! Dad's been running around the house with a sweatshirt on and a towel wrapped around his neck. I've been drinking coffee, tea, and soup all day. More Fun!

This alert is sure queer. There are guards all over the place, and everyone is running around with guns on. The sirens keep blowing on all sides of us. Wonder why we haven't had a black out— Did the dishes, listened to the radio (music and of course, The Shadow) and then got around to doing my homework. Took a bath and went to bed.

Wonder if we'll be at war by this time next month. . . . I certainly do hope not. Especially not with the Japs!

• Monday, December 1, 1941

Ah joy to the cold weather. I hope it keeps up until Christmas. Wish it would snow or something. Everyone at school was, of course, freezing, but I felt wonderful. First chance I've had to wear the jacket

In the early days of December 1941, several thousand miles away from Jim Wood's small town in West Virginia, a seventeen-year-old girl named Ginger, a high school senior living at Hickam Field, Hawaii, was keeping a diary.

I got for my birthday. Kay was absent and Gaye has an infected hand. That sure must have been a wild picnic their homeroom gave on Friday. Had to write another dumb theme—this time on "How Football Promotes Unity." I swear! It took me a whole study hall and from 6:30 'till ten, AND record period tomorrow to finish it. (I hope I finish it tomorrow!!) It's the worst I've done so far.

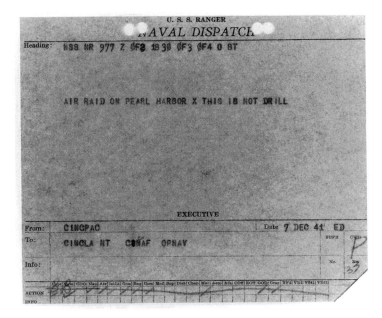

• **Tuesday, December 2, 1941**

Finished my theme in record period. Added a last paragraph and brought the sum total of words up to 196. It's supposed to be less than two hundred and more than one hundred and ninety. I guess it came out perfect, except that most of it is just that—words!!

Sorority meeting night. It was my turn to take us, but Mom and Dad were going out, so . . . Kay got her car after a battle with her family. Voted on new members. Certainly came out odd. The people I expected to get in didn't. Ann did, however, and I'm the one who put her name in so that's something. Talked about Christmas basket. Next meeting is next Tuesday. It's really going to be a battle then. So close!!

• **Wednesday, December 3, 1941**

More things happened today! Number 1: Mrs F LIKED my theme and sent it in to the contest. It's about the first one I've written that hasn't been the worst in the class. Number 2: No more music lessons. My teacher had to quit because of Doctors orders, and the other two teachers' schedules were filled. Guess I am forced to take a holiday for a while. No. 3: The "Advertiser" is going to take our pictures making choir robes tomorrow. More fun. No. 4: Finally got around to buying Mom's gravy bowl. It's yellow. No. 5: Went to a technicolor movie. "Dive Bomber" with Errol Flynn. Very good!

The aircraft carrier **Ranger** *was at sea in the Atlantic in the early days of December 1941, heading back toward Norfolk, Virginia, after a stint on ocean patrol. Aboard, the men were probably already making out their Christmas cards, and their loved ones at home would be preparing Christmas gift packages and sending them off early enough for the soldiers to receive them by the holidays. The cards and the packages would arrive on time, but the context in which they would be received would be dramatically altered by the message to the* **Ranger** *depicted here.*

★ ★ ★

A little girl opens her presents in Washington, D.C., on Christmas Day 1941. But it might as well be anywhere in the United States as Americans tried to celebrate the first Christmas of the war, less than three weeks after the attack on Pearl Harbor. While the tree and the presents will be there for each succeeding Christmas over the next three years, many fathers and brothers will not.

☆ ☆ ☆

• **Thursday, December 4, 1941**

There was an all-school assembly second period so we didn't have any English. She [the teacher] was going to make us write an application for a job in class. Now we get to do it for homework. The other classes have to read theirs in class, and we don't. Wrote mine in the library instead of going to assembly. There is a new girl at school. She's from California and she's very cute. Seems like a swell girl, too.

Finished up the Christmas cards so Mom could get them off on the boat tomorrow. She got twenty-five prints of a picture she took of us kids so she could send them to some of her best friends. Lucky people!

• **Friday, December 5, 1941**

Ah! at last 'tis Friday. Nothing of import happened except that the second year French class decided to use the pin I designed. They didn't even look at any others. I guess they liked mine because it was so nice and inexpensive and simple.

Kay and I are going to usher at the Community Theater play at Punahou tomorrow evening. Patsy got us seats for today and everything got all messed up. Pat finally gave them to some friends of hers and everyone was happy. Put an ad for a class ring on Mom's bureau. I hope she takes the hint!! There's a terrific gale blowing. I'm going to wash my hair tomorrow if it kills me!!

• **Saturday, December 6, 1941**

Washed my hair finally. It's warm again, so it dried real fast. Read the paper and then it was time to eat lunch. Listened to the Shriner's football game over the radio. The University beat Willamatte 20–6. I spent all afternoon reading funny books and trying to get our transportation figured out for tonight. Finally fixed it so Hester took us and Dad brought us home. We (Kay and I) were ushering at Punahou for the play "Mr. and Mrs. North." It was pretty good. We got home about ten of twelve and I'm very sleepy. Lani invited us to dinner Tuesday.

• **Sunday, December 7, 1941**

BOMBED! 8:00 in the morning. Unknown attacker so far! Pearl Harbor in flames! Also Hickam hanger [sic] line. So far no houses bombed here.

5 of 11:00. We've left the post. It got too hot. The PX is in flames, also the barracks. We made a dash during a lull. Left everything we own there. Found out the attackers are Japs. Rats!!! A couple of non-com's houses demolished. Hope Kay is O.K. We're at M's. It's all so sudden and surprising I can't believe it's really happening. It's awful. School is discontinued until further notice . . . there goes my graduation.

Churchill Speaks to Americans on Christmas Eve

On December 23, 1941, Prime Minister Winston Churchill, his face cherubic and pink-tinged, a cigar pressed between his lips, and glasses stuffed in his coat breast-pocket, met with President Franklin D. Roosevelt. The two talked war, plotting strategy and coordination between the United States and Britain against the Axis powers. The following afternoon, Mr. Churchill and Mr. Roosevelt participated in the annual lighting of the national Christmas tree south of the White House. The Prime Minister delivered a Christmas greeting to the people of America.

I spend this anniversary and festival far from my country, far from my family, and yet I cannot truthfully say that I feel far from home. Whether it be the ties of blood on my mother's side, or the friendships I have developed here over many years of active life, or the commanding sentiment of comradeship in the common cause of great races who speak the same language and to a very large extent worship the same altars and pursue the same ideals. Whichever it may be—or all of them together—I cannot feel myself a stranger here in the center of the summit of these United States. I feel a sense of unity and fraternal association which, through all your kindness, convinces me that I have a right to sit at your fireside and share your Christmas joys.

This is a strange Christmas Eve. Almost the whole world is locked in deadly struggle. Armed with the most terrible weapons which science can devise, the nations advance upon each other. Ill would it be for us this Christmastide if we were not sure that no greed for the lands or wealth of any other people has led us to the field. That no vulgar ambition, no sordid lust for material gain at the expense of others had led us to the field. Here in the midst of war, raging and roaring about us over all the lands and seas, creeping nearer to our hearts and homes. Here amidst all these tumults, we have the peace of the spirit in each cottage home and in every heart.

Therefore we may cast aside, for this night at least, the cares and dangers which beset us, and make the children happy in a world of storm. Here then, for one night only, each home throughout the English-speaking world, should be a brightly lighted island of happiness and peace. Let the children have their night of fun and laughter; let the gifts of Father Christmas delight their thoughts; let us share to the full in their unstinted pleasure, before we turn again to the stern tasks in the year that lies before us. But now, by our sacrifice and daring, these same children shall not be robbed of their inheritance, or denied the right to live in a free and decent world.

And so, in God's mercy, a Happy Christmas to you all. ☆

In Norfolk, Virginia, news that the United States had been plunged into war sobers the mood of the shipmates on the USS **Washington.** *When the radio plays "The Star-Spangled Banner," the men all stand and sing. They realize that immediate action on the high seas is ahead. A few days later, just before Christmas 1941, a writer for the ship's weekly newsletter,* **Cougar Scream,** *talks about duty, love, and sacrifice.*

GREATER LOVE HATH NO MAN

THE KNOWLEDGE OF a catastrophe cannot be comprehended within the immediate moments of its announcement. It is one thing to know—it is another thing to realize. We all heard the shocking narration of death, disaster, and destruction as relayed from Pearl Harbor last Sunday. We know it took place. But do we realize its significance?

It is difficult to realize that some of our shipmates of former days and duties are dead; that others are seriously wounded. It seems incredible that ships-of-the-line have been sunk. And to watery graves went men who manned those ships. Those men wore the uniform of their country by their own choice, through their own free will. When each solemnly swore: "I do solemnly swear that I will bear true faith and allegiance to the United States of America, and that I will serve them honestly and faithfully against all their enemies whomsoever, and that I will obey the orders of the President of the United States and the orders of the Officers appointed over me, according to the rules and articles for the government of the Navy," he assumed a grave responsibility. That responsibility can be shouldered only by the security of a sense of duty. Duty is any assigned service. Duty is founded upon love or upon fear. A fearful man could not freely undertake this responsibility. He would have to be forced into it because he would be afraid of its obligations. That rules out fear and leaves love only. It might be a love of country; a love of home and family—and their attendant preservation; a love of an ideal and the subsequent pride of maintaining the high standards of that ideal.

Love and Duty have one common denominator—Sacrifice. Both require it; both demand it. Without sacrifice there can be no duty. Sacrifice is in proportion to love. The more we love something, the less willing are we to part with it. Since self-preservation is the first law of nature, it follows that we are least willing to part with our life. To part with life requires a tremendous sacrifice and such a sacrifice demands a tremendous love. Therefore, "Greater love hath no man than he lay down his life for his friends."

The men of last Sunday who could not be bribed by the Grim Reaper to desert their posts; the men who placed duty, love, and honor above fear, life, and dishonor; the men whom the Angel of Death

After a look at these headlines on Christmas morning, it took some effort to be merry, and the prospects were not good for a happy New Year. There was still a reasonable fear that the U.S. mainland might be attacked—witness the story in column seven of a Japanese submarine torpedoing a freighter just off the California coast. In November 1942, a Japanese plane would actually drop bombs on an Oregon forest, and German U-boats wreaked havoc on Allied ships off the East Coast throughout the early part of the war. One U-boat even landed spies on a Long Island beach (they were eventually caught). By the end of January 1942, five and a half million Americans had volunteered for civil defense to counter such dangers.

⋆ ⋆ ⋆

The New York Times.

FREE FRENCH SEIZE ST. PIERRE AND MIQUELON; TWO MORE ENEMY LANDINGS MENACE MANILA; WAKE LOST AFTER 14-DAY STAND BY TINY FORCE

tapped on the shoulder and who, without flinching, returned Death's gaze as they stood by their stations—those men were our shipmates of former days and duties; those men laid down their lives for their friends. Greater love could no man have.

We of the WASHINGTON pause with bowed heads to pay homage to our gallant brothers who have "given the last full measure of devotion." May their souls rest in peace through the infinite mercy and love of Almighty God.

Invocation for Victory

From the White House on Christmas Day 1941, President Roosevelt lamented the beast of war, "the evil thing," but called on the nation to unsheathe its sword in the cause of "Honor, Truth and Justice." This was, he said, a war for "that conviction of the dignity and brotherhood of man which Christmas Day signifies." The President invited the Reverend Joseph M. Corrigan, the rector of Catholic University, to deliver an invocation. Across the world, Christian ministers on the Axis side would also invoke the blessing of God in their shared cause. But Reverend Corrigan and others at the White House that day called on God to strike down the "false leaders," those who mocked the Christmas message.

LORD, GOD, Father of us all, keep us in Thy Providence as war and Christmas meet in our Fatherland.

Hear a united people, girded for battle, dedicate themselves to the Peace of Christmas nor find strangeness in our words.

All the material resources with which Thou hast blessed our Native Land we consecrate here to the dread tasks of war.

On land and water, in the sky above, in the depths of the sea, shall the despoilers of liberty find us hurtling to prove that the things for which men gladly die shall have, as always they had, the unfailing loyalty, the untiring defense, the victorious aggression of the brave and the free.

We pray for all who hold power over human life; therefore, for the leader we have chosen. Keep him in Thy grace, through this stress of war, strong and tender, wise and fearless, nor let his hand be stayed until he can sheathe his nation's sword in a peace of honor, truth and justice.

We pray also for the leader of our great ally [Winston Churchill], the man of tears and blood and sweat—and patience. Put prudence and daring and the will to wait through failure without faltering into their compacts and planning that the united efforts of total war prove the quickest leveling of the path to peace and freedom.

Father of all men, keep us mindful of all who suffer in the world today. Thy children, our brothers, and purge our hearts of all hate, save hate for evil deeds of false leaders, who, having defiled their people's freedom, have made the Peace of Good Will a mockery this Christmas night upon this earth.

Oh, God that Thou art not mocked. We wait Thy hour of Peace, even as we advance the grim weapon of war. Bless all who pray for Thy Peace and do Thou strengthen us who give battle for its victory through Christ Our Lord. Amen.

Santa gets into the spirit of the times in this cartoon, guiding his reindeer into a V for victory. No symbol was more omnipresent during these years than this simple letter. It was first used in 1940 by a Belgian refugee, broadcasting from abroad to his occupied homeland. He called for his countrymen to mark a V (standing for Victoire) on walls to show defiance to the Germans. On the radio, this symbol was represented by the opening notes of Beethoven's Fifth Symphony because the Morse code for the letter was dot-dot-dot-dash, evoking the accents on those notes. Winston Churchill's "V for victory" sign, flashed with his fingers, became a familiar sight. In America a stamp carried the symbol, and Tiffany's sold a V-shaped diamond brooch, priced at $5,000.

★ ★ ★

V FOR VICTORY

It's Christmas, and at the Greyhound terminal in Washington, D.C., it seems that everyone wants to rush home for the holidays at the same time. Barely two weeks after Pearl Harbor, the fact of the war has sunk in, lives are being changed enormously, and many people can easily anticipate further serious disruptions to what they had thought of as their everyday existence. But with casualty lists at this point nothing like they are going to become, and even young men already drafted not yet sent overseas, there is still time for one last almost-normal Christmas.

☆ ☆ ☆

Dedicated to America—
A Poem by Alfred Noyes

For Great Britain, Christmas 1941 was not the beginning of the war; that nation had already suffered grievously. As the bombs blasted Pearl Harbor and as America lined up on the Allied side, many in Great Britain realized that a strong United States might turn the tide of the war. The esteemed English poet Alfred Noyes, author of "The Highwayman," dedicated a poem to America at the holiday season.

CHRISTMAS—1941

Who dreamed that earth's one light was now in danger,
    The eternal drama but an idle tale,
While Herod dreads the memory of that manger
    Which challenges his might, and shall prevail—

Through endless time shall Rachel not remember
    Her children drowned beneath the midnight seas;
Or freedom's land forget, this bleak December,
    Christ and his mother, once, were refugees—

May we, who in our own wide frontiers gather
    All races to one freedom, kneel this night,
Praying one prayer, repeating one "Our Father . . ."
    Hoping one hope, and cherishing one light,

Till all men cry "good news!"—there is no way,
No truth, no light, but leads thro' Christmas Day.

"I'll never forget . . . Pearl Harbor"

The great decisions and events that turn history around always look a little less neat and comprehensible when seen from the ground up. Fred Edinger saw Pearl Harbor, one of those events, as it happened, without knowing exactly what was going on or where it would finally fit into the scheme of things. All he knew was that on a lazy Sunday morning in Hawaii less than three weeks before Christmas, without warning, unfriendly planes were definitely shooting in his direction. Here, in the first minutes of American participation in World War II, he was also already experiencing the often written-about "absurdity" of war. With the bullets flying—and for all he knew, men dying—he had to fulfill his duty to look after the base's sickbook.

WE HAD JUST BEEN on an alert from the last of November to the 6th of December, but we went to bed December 6th not giving a thought of what the next day might hold for us. The next day being Sunday, we could sleep all morning if we wished. We usually would get up around 7 o'clock and eat breakfast. So 7 o'clock found me in the mess hall

A Marine Remembers the Common Cause

Edward Vila was sixteen years old when the news of Pearl Harbor reached his house in New York City. Edward's mother gathered her three sons around for hugs; she sensed that the war would touch the family. Later, as a marine, Edward was wounded in Okinawa. Although he returned to his family's New York apartment leaning on a cane, he, along with his brothers, survived the war. For his mother, it was a dream realized "that her sons would come home again."

It wasn't a green and white Christmas in New York City that year. Patriotism brought out the red, white and blue in my neighborhood. We weren't Italian-American, Irish-American, German-American, Spanish-American, Russian-American, Black-American or Jewish-American anymore. We were all Americans bound together for a common cause, willing to fight our country's battles at home and in the battlefields.

I observed displays in neighbors' windows, small rectangular banners with red borders and a white center. These banners represented a family member in the service. A blue star in the center of the white field represented each member on active duty. A gold star signified a family member who was killed on active duty at Pearl Harbor or on some distant shore.

Mothers weren't just giving up rationed items that were needed by the armed forces—such as food, clothing, gasoline, tires. Their children were putting their lives on the line for their country and home to silence the drums of war. ✶

enjoying some eggs (fried sunny side up). I had hardly started to eat when we heard planes diving around some distance away, and explosions take place (this was at Schofield Barracks). "Well," someone said, "that's the Air Corps doing some maneuvering again," and we kept on eating.

Soon someone comes in from outside and says, "that's not our planes; there are red circles on them!" We just couldn't believe it, but the next moment alert was blown, (meanwhile planes began flying over and strafing our barracks). Boy, what a rush!

Our rifles as usual were locked in racks, and ammunition was in the supply room. Well, we finally got our rifles. I happened to step outside and saw a large amount of smoke in the vicinity of Wheeler Field, main target in our area. While the other fellows took machine guns and B.A.R.'s up on the roof, it was my duty to get the 1st Sergeant, who lives up the road a way. I met him coming down. He says, "What's the hurry; this is the real thing; take your time." My next duty was to take the sickbook to an appointed place. Imagine carrying a sickbook around in the first moments of World War No. 2.

The planes were only around our barracks about half an hour, and I believe our boys got one of them; or one of us. We were very confused.

We were soon out in trucks bound for the beach defenses of which we had a designated place. On our way we passed Pearl Harbor. I could see very little but smoke; how many ships were hit I cannot say but it sure looked bad. Then, as we went through Honolulu, the civilians sure cheered us (first time, too, since I had been in Hawaii— 9 months).

We soon arrived at our beach positions and set up defenses; a task we worked at day and night for almost 6 months. We were certainly scared those first few months. I never knew it could be so hard to stay awake—and the penalty for sleeping on post is no joke. We fired at most anything, including mongeese, of which there are plenty.

★ ★ ★

LEFT. These sailors are having a Christmas Eve dinner in Williamsburg, the capital of colonial Virginia, courtesy of Mrs. John D. Rockefeller, Jr. In 1926 her husband agreed to help finance the restoration of Williamsburg. Whether they remain in the North Atlantic to fight the German U-boat menace to Allied convoys, or sail to take on the Japanese Empire, just now expanding in the Pacific, these sailors will need the memory of fellowship and good cheer at one last peaceful Christmas, for they have a long and bloody road ahead of them.

In the Aftermath of Pearl Harbor —
Mele Kalikimaka!

CHRISTMAS IN HAWAII. What visions that brings to mind: Santa on a surfboard; Santa under a coconut tree; Santa surrounded by Hula girls in grass skirts. But this was December 25, 1941, and peace on earth was just a dream. That year, in the "paradise of the Pacific," Christmas loomed gray and grim. We were still reeling from the cruel blow the Japanese had dealt us December 7.

Told to be ready for evacuation with little notice, we had kept Christmas purchases to a minimum. A scrappy, stringy Poinsettia stood on a table under the window where our three-year-old, Mary Jane, hung her stocking with the sure confidence of the young that Santa would find and fill it.

The table was placed under a window where I had stood that December day, watching bombs rain down on Pearl Harbor's unsuspecting men and ships. The same window where that evening I had watched the sky blossom with lights from tracer bullets aiming for something I didn't want to imagine.

A blackout had been ordered, so we sat in the dark, with only sporadic reports from our tiny radio for news and for company. Around 10 o'clock, the radio warned, "Everyone stop your cars, turn off your lights. Pearl Harbor is being bombed again."

The radio was silent again and we had no news at all. Sleep was impossible, and as I waited, the radio started up again, and I heard "Japanese are landing on the windward side of the island and are coming ashore, climbing over the dead bodies of our defenders."

I had no way of knowing whether it was true. It only added to the terror the day had brought. The radio went silent; the long night was over.

My husband, William J. (Red) Coleman, was stationed aboard the light cruiser, Raleigh. It was moored just ahead of the Utah on the other side of Ford Island, away from battleship row. It was three days before I learned he was safe; it was December 11 before he was able to reach home. His ship sustained bomb and torpedo hits.

Martial law had been declared; civilians were asked to stay off the streets, and news was censored. Wives would gather to exchange any bits

At Pearl Harbor on December 7, 1941, Agnes P. Coleman watched the frightening sight of bombs and tracer bullets and the billowing smoke rising from the waters where her husband was stationed on a cruiser. For a time she feared that he was lost.

of information that came our way. Rumors in the Navy are commonly called "scuttlebutt" and are unreliable, but we had no alternatives.

To hear that so many of our men were lost was devastating. We heard the Arizona had capsized and sunk; the Utah sunk; the Oklahoma was hit; the Maryland, Tennessee, Pennsylvania and the West Virginia were all hit and damaged or lost.

We listened in dismay and disbelief. I wrote the names down on an envelope, using shorthand to conceal what I had written.

The days were short and the blacked-out nights were unbearably long that December. We'd sit out on the patio at twilight and listen to the plaintive sounds of someone in the distance play Hawaiian songs on an accordion.

Back inside there were only the radio and bed. We had a closet with an overhead light, so after Mary Jane was sleeping, I'd sit in there with the door closed, to read the newspaper and write letters home until I had to come out for air. I still have the December 7 and 8 editions of *The Honolulu Star-Bulletin.*

One day we gathered at a school to be issued gas masks. Fortunately, they went unused.

It was mid-December, and Red was able to get home for a short time every fourth day. We knew his ship was being made ready to sail and that each time together might be our last.

No, the musician is not part of some celebrity troop of entertainers. Her name is Joyce Wilcos, and she will probably never meet Bob Hope or appear on the radio. But for these patients spending Christmas at the Base Hospital, Camp Robinson, Arkansas, she and her accordion are a Christmas gift to be treasured. Because of her, Christmas on the ward will be a little less bleak, a little more endurable.

✩ ✩ ✩

★ 1941 ★

There wasn't the usual Christmas spirit in the air. Feelings of "good will toward men" were definitely missing as we thought of the enemy. Christmas was not our main concern. All that mattered was that we three were alive and well, and for the moment, together.

Christmas Day we were up early. Presents and cards had finally arrived from the States, and Mary Jane's delight in what Santa had brought recovered the season's glow. Later in the day my husband came home, and as he bounded up the steps with a big smile, suddenly and miraculously, it was a joyous Christmas in Hawaii.

Mele Kalikimaka! [Merry Christmas]

The men stationed at Camp Langdon in Portsmouth, New Hampshire, have a special guest for Christmas: Jimmy Durante, star of vaudeville, Broadway musicals, Hollywood comedies, and radio. His raspy voice and engaging, lively personality were intimately familiar to this generation of Americans.

★ ★ ★

26

As war gripped America for the first time since 1917, a reporter for the **New York Times** *looked at the Christmas season from several perspectives.*

TITANIC WORLD EVENTS cast their shadow over the spirit of the holiday throughout the land. Christmas lights blinked from country homes and city skyscraper apartment windows—for blackouts had not come generally to America yet—and little children went to bed last night in excited anticipation of what the morning would bring them. But over it all, in the minds of all sober-thinking citizens, was the unshakable, ever-present realization of the job that must be done before the world can laugh again.

Though the city's great department stores and glittering shops were packed yesterday with last-minute shoppers in search of gay and frivolous things; though post-office receipts broke a ten-year record, and trains, buses and planes were jammed with holiday travelers; though traditional Christmas carols were heard and hymns rang out from the churches at midnight, few persons could forget that this was America at war.

The realization was present in the Christmas message from Mayor La Guardia to the people of the city, in which he warned that "no one can fathom the deviltry of the Nazi command." It was present in the wording of Police Commissioner Valentine's greeting to his men, in which he expressed his utmost confidence in our ability to cope with any and all problems. The telephone company's proclamation asking the public not to make long-distance calls today because the lines must be kept open for defense use was another reminder.

The civilian volunteer "spotters," who scanned the skies last night for enemy planes, remembered it too. So did the young pilots from Mitchell Field, many of them far from their home States, as they droned over New York's coastline, on the alert.

Thus it was all over the world: In Washington, where President Roosevelt and Prime Minister Churchill, lighting a Christmas tree on the White House lawn, looked out over a sea of faces and addressed their pleas to "fellow-workers in the cause of freedom"; in Vatican City, where Pope Pius XII gravely propounded a five-point plan for the future peace of the world; in Bethlehem, where the pilgrims and the refugees of the world trudged along blacked-out roads to solemn services at the Church of the Nativity.

In Japan the people planned to celebrate today—not the Christian Christmas but the fifteenth anniversary of the succession of the Emperor Hirohito; in Manila, brave, beleaguered Filipinos, a Christian people for 400 years, sorrowfully curtailed their midnight masses in their hour of great danger; already they were counting their dead.

Across the English Channel German long-range guns shelled the Straits of Dover for fifteen minutes, but in one town villagers contemptuously ignored the shelling and went on singing Christmas carols. General Charles de Gaulle broadcast a message of good cheer to the children of France, and Radio Rome, broadcasting to North America, shrilled "a merry Christmas to all who realize that Mr. Churchill is the man responsible for this war!" In crushed France, the aged Marshal Pétain spoke pessimistically of peace "farther off than ever," and in Russia, Libya, China, Singapore, and the remote isles of the Pacific men slaughtered one another.

It was a far cry, though, from Christmas of 1940, and many observers thought that, despite hard days to come, the situation on the whole seemed brighter for men of good will. Last Christmas a million Londoners were living underground, fearing momentary invasion; in the Reich, a spokesman—Marshal Walther von Braunchitsch—was thundering that the English Channel would be no more effective than the Maginot Line, and America's rising new Army still was pretty much on paper. Ironically enough, it was on December 24, 1940, that a pact was signed between Japan and Thailand; that pact pledged "amity and mutual respect for territory."

For the first time in fifty years yesterday the local Weather Bureau omitted until late afternoon all forecasts of Christmas weather—that, too, was due to wartime restrictions—and last night gave out an official prediction of fair and somewhat colder.

On this Christmas Eve, the war was still young enough for a soldier to mark the number of days into the conflict on his diary page. There would be well over a thousand more days before the Japanese would surrender aboard the battleship **Missouri.** Meanwhile, the Philippine islands, where Ron Wood-house is stationed, are not safe. The Japanese attacked them as well as Pearl Harbor on December 7. Manila, the capital of the Philippines, will fall on January 2 after a nine-day siege. On April 9, Japan will capture the Bataan Peninsula, and the island of Corregidor will surrender on May 6, the survivors of the battle forced on a "Death March." It will be October 1944 before General Douglas MacArthur makes his triumphant return to the Philippines.

★ ★ ★

This Christmas image was a perfect symbol for some of the deprivations and inconveniences that Americans were already facing early in the conflict. Christmas lights in general, and the Star of Bethlehem in particular, represented not only joy, peace, and things spiritual, they also stood for the opposite of the effect achieved by the already onerous blackout rules. Blackouts were instituted so that enemy planes would not have lights to guide them toward their targets. The federal government set up an Office of Civilian Defense, but requirements that civilians dim, turn out, or cover their lights by putting up opaque black curtains were enforced on the local level. In big cities, there were wardens assigned to each block to ensure compliance.

★ ★ ★

A Family Waits

Dear Ray:

I'll write and write—just like you've answered my letter 'cause I think you must be getting better. I hope well enough to enjoy Christmas. It's raining here—imagine—Thursday is Christmas and no snow. I love rain—but not when it should be snowing. To me that's what makes it Christmas—the lights from the trees inside the houses reflecting on the snow. The creak of tires on the cars riding by. The snow on your eye lashes—and the dear little children who pop you in the kisser with a snow ball when you least expect it.

I have a friend who loves dogs and every year she gets so many Christmas cards with dogs on them. This year you'd be surprised at the number of cards we've received with boats on them. Not because we like them so much tho—it's because of you—you know we've talked about you so much—and believe me it's all good!!

I don't suppose you'd care for a card with a boat on it. Bet you're sorta fed up on 'em—right?

I hope you're not disappointed 'cause you didn't get a Christmas package—we don't know where you are, how you are, or if you are (sounds like that song "All Alone," doesn't it?) well enough to enjoy what we . . . wanted to send you . . .

Except for you—I've got my Christmas shopping done—Got a nice Paradise Fruit cake for your Ma and Pa . . . How about you Ray? Could you enjoy one? Or would a plate of mushrooms fried in butter taste better—or perhaps a fried cheese sandwich? 'Member when you told me they were swell—and a couple of days later you confessed you didn't like them? You are a perfect liar—and a nice one!

Got to leave room for Leon.

Alice

Hi—Ya? Ma was knitting a sweater for the Red Cross and her knitting needle broke. I haven't much room to write anymore so, so—long.

Leon

After receiving a short telegram from the U.S. government on December 11 informing them that Ray Woods, seaman second class on the USS **Pennsylvania,** *had been wounded in the Pearl Harbor attack, his family waited for additional news. How severe were the injuries? Where was he now? On December 21, Ray's sister-in-law Alice Woods, racked with uncertainty and concern, wrote to the wounded sailor. A welcome response from Ray would arrive eight days later; he had survived.*

Private First Class Oscar E. O'Guin is getting that warm holiday feeling despite finding himself at Camp Pershing in Iceland at Christmas. It had been barely two decades since Iceland had achieved its independence from Denmark when it experienced a "friendly" invasion by British troops in 1940. The British needed to set up bases to secure routes for their convoys in the North Atlantic. Americans followed in July 1941, and the war's peak numbered 45,000. Their air bases allowed them to carry out effective attacks against the German U-boats.

☆ ☆ ☆

1942

☆ ☆ ☆

AMERICA WAS a very different place in 1942 than it had
been a year earlier. Across the country citizens began to
change eating and driving habits to accommodate growing
wartime shortages. As plants and businesses retooled for war,
Americans also began to change jobs, many, including thousands of women, beginning factory jobs for the first time.
Americans began to listen carefully to news reports of battles
and front lines in places they never knew existed. At train and
bus stations, they said good-bye to friends and lovers who
were heading to those places.

For some the changes were profound. Some received telegrams informing them of devastating personal losses. For others the changes came en masse. In February, Congress advised President Roosevelt that because of the Japanese attack on Pearl Harbor two months earlier Americans of Japanese descent should be locked up so they could not oppose the U.S. war effort. Within months, more than 100,000 Japanese-Americans were placed in remote prison camps. Some would remain there for three years.

The war began to produce legends and stories that would survive generations. In January Navy pilot David F. Mason, noticing a surfaced Japanese submarine in the South Pacific, dropped his depth charges and radioed in the result: "Sighted sub, sank same."

The people struggled to take their minds off the war. They relaxed with the Glenn Miller recording of "I've Got a Gal in Kalamazoo" and lined up at theaters to see Walt Disney's *Bambi* and *Holiday Inn* starring Bing Crosby, who sang Irving Berlin's "White Christmas."

Popular entertainment also began to reflect the war. In a memorable slap at the Germans, Spike Jones and the City Slickers made the pop chart with "De Führer's Face"; on Thanksgiving Day 1942 the Academy Award–winning motion picture *Casablanca*, starring Humphrey Bogart and Ingrid Bergman, had its world premiere in New York City; in late December Bob Hope agreed to entertain U.S. airmen in Alaska, the first of his many famous shows at Christmas for American armed forces around the world; and Clark Gable, now in the army, shaved off his famous mustache.

The Three Unwise Men

Here the three Axis leaders, Emperor Hirohito, Adolf Hitler, and Benito Mussolini, are no match for the Christmas star.

★ ★ ★

After a series of bitter defeats in battle, especially in the Philippines and in the Java Sea, the American forces began to assert power. In June in the Battle of Midway, they gained their first major victory over Japan in the Pacific theater. Later in the year, the naval battle of Guadalcanal in the Solomon Islands began. Although both sides suffered heavy losses, the Americans won a major victory over the Japanese, whose forces on Guadalcanal were left virtually isolated. In November U.S. and British amphibious operations began in North Africa—its leaders: Admiral Sir Andrew Cunningham and Lieutenant General Dwight D. Eisenhower.

Typical Day for the Anti-Tank Section

Dec. 25th—Special mission to Gafsa returned to Feriana at 0730, Bn S-1 returned at 0830 after reporting results at French Hq at Gafsa. On reaching Gafsa on the night of the 24th at 1900, the mission consisting of Capt Hughes, Lt Honecker, 2nd section of the 3rd Bn Anti-Tank platoon, and one section of Ammunition and Pioneer Platoon proceeded to Sened where they were met by Lt Buttolph and 12 men of Company "M." The mission of the Anti-Tank section was to proceed along the road, Gafsa, Sened, Maknassy, to utilize the closest possible range of the town of Maknassy, and open fire south two Anti-Tank guns, on the town, firing for approximately five minutes, and then withdrawing as quickly as possible to Gafsa. Lt Buttolph and his patrol were to secure the route mentioned above and also provide local security for the Anti-Tank guns. Both patrols left Sened at 2230, at twenty minute intervals, over very muddy, and rough roads. The advance patrol detrucked at a point five miles west of Maknassy and proceeded on foot, followed by the Bn Anti-Tank section. The patrol moved forward to a point one mile west of Maknassy, where gun positions were selected. At the moment the guns advanced from rear of column to their positions, all enemy guns, both anti-tank and automatic weapons opened fire on all roads leading from the town. This enemy fire lasted for about five minutes. Because of unsuitable terrain, and a lack of cover for anti-tank guns our guns did not fire. (Our mission was solely to create confusion in the town: this was done without firing a shot). Our route of approach to the town was under heavy enemy anti-tank gun fire, so the mission withdrew immediately. Mission successful without expenditure of men, vehicles or ammunition. The same night a patrol lead by Lieutenant Megrail consisting of three men from Company "L" and four Pioneer men with a mission of laying mines and cutting enemy telephone wires, at El Hafey southeast of El Guettar, attempted to accomplish their mission. They were fired on by 2 anti-tank guns, 4 machine guns, and approximately seventy riflemen, that were occupying an outlying outpost. Throughout the evening, our patrols succeeded in harassing and exciting the enemy outposts with no damage to themselves. Otherwise Christmas day was enjoyed by all.

For some troops on the front lines, Christmas meant at least a short respite for singing, sharing stories, mail from home, gifts, and religious ceremony. For others, there was no cessation of battle. For the Third Battalion Anti-Tank Section patrolling the muddy roads near a town in Tunisia, North Africa, on Christmas Day 1942, it meant cutting telephone wires, laying mines, and opening fire on enemy posts. For the GI keeping the unit section journal, the occurrence of Christmas was no more than an ironic afterthought.

A Fireside Chat on Christmas

One of the great qualities Franklin Roosevelt brought to the presidency was an unparalleled ability to communicate as a confidant to the American people in times of intense uncertainty. He did it during the Great Depression. And now, with the nation gripped in all-out war, the President's fireside chats, drawing millions around their radio sets across the country, became a source of comfort. The nation was family and the President offered personal Christmas greetings.

THIS YEAR, my friends, I am speaking on Christmas Eve not to this gathering at the White House only but to all of the citizens of our nation, to the men and women serving in our American armed forces and also to those who wear the uniforms of the other United Nations.

General MacArthur Wires Christmas Greetings

Throughout the war, the U.S. military leadership realized that their success on the battlefield depended on the success of the wartime industries back home. On December 22, 1942, General Douglas MacArthur, Supreme Commander of Allied Forces in the Southwest Pacific, sent Christmas greetings to workers in numerous individual war plants throughout the United States, including General Cable Corporation of New York.

TO THE MEN AND WOMEN OF GENERAL CABLE CORPORATION:

ON THIS SACRED DAY OF OUR LORD WE, THE SOLDIERS ON THE FIRING LINE, GIVE THANKS TO YOU SOLDIERS ON THE PRODUCTION LINE FOR THE SINEWS OF WAR THAT MAKE VICTORY POSSIBLE. WE ARE DEDICATING THIS CHRISTMAS DAY TO THE DEFEAT OF OUR ENEMIES—YES. THIS CHRISTMAS DAY, THE DAY AFTER AND EVERY DAY THEREAFTER UNTIL WE ESTABLISH PEACE ON EARTH AND GOOD WILL TO MEN.

MACARTHUR ★

I give you a message of cheer. I cannot say "Merry Christmas," for I think constantly of those thousands of soldiers and sailors who are in actual combat throughout the world, but I can express to you my thought that this is a happier Christmas than last year, happier in the sense that the forces of darkness stand against us with less confidence in the success of their evil ways.

To you who toil in industry and in offices, toil for the common cause of helping to win the war, I send a message of cheer, that you can well continue to sacrifice without recrimination and with a look of Christmas cheer, a kindly spirit toward your fellow men.

To you who serve in uniform I also send a message of cheer, that you are in the thoughts of your families, your friends at home, and that Christmas prayers follow you wherever you may be.

To all Americans I say that loving your neighbor as we love ourselves is not enough, that we as a nation and as individuals will please God best by showing regard for the laws of God. There is no better way at this Christmastide or any other time of fostering good will toward man than by first fostering good will toward God. If we love Him, we will keep his Commandments.

In sending Christmas greetings to the armed forces and the merchant sailors of the United States, we include therein our pride in their bravery on the fighting fronts and on all the seas. But we remember in our greetings and in our pride those other men who guard remote islands and bases and will, in all probability, never come into active combat with the

For the First Family, as for other American families, Christmas was a family affair. Here several generations of Roosevelts are posed in front of their tree at the White House. First Lady Eleanor Roosevelt is seated at the left next to the President's mother, Sara. Standing are two of Roosevelt's sons, from the left, Franklin, Jr., and John and a son-in-law. Four of the Roosevelt boys were in the service in World War II, making the family in the White House an exemplar of the kinds of sacrifices that so many other Americans were making.

★ ★ ★

common enemy. They are stationed in distant places, far from home. They have few contacts with the outside world, and I want them to know that their work is essential to the conduct of this war, essential to the ultimate victory, and that we have not forgotten them.

It is significant that tomorrow—Christmas Day—our plants and factories will be stilled. That is not true of the other holidays that we have long been accustomed to celebrate. On all other holidays the work goes on, gladly, for the winning of the war.

So Christmas Day becomes the only holiday in all the year.

I like to think that this is so because Christmas is a holy day. May all that it stands for live and grow through all the years.

Opening a Department Store's Family Mail

Hello gang at A & S!

Today received your September 15 letter and hasten to answer it and correct the address, in case someone should write to me here in Australia. As shown on this letterhead, my address is now with a higher headquarters. Sorry I can't go into details, but the censor might have to wield his scissors.

If the spelling, grammar, layout, or content of this letter is slightly below A & S standards, then picture me, writing this, swatting mosquitoes in the rain with the humidity close to saturation and the sweat pouring out. We are enjoying (?) our rainy season here now, which means rain, and blistering sun, steam, humidity, rain, etc. Nothing like the air conditioning I once took for granted at A & S.

You ask for suggestions as to what the service men would like for gifts. You certainly came to the right place, so sharpen your pencil and note carefully: (1) A certified copy of the peace treaty ending this war. (2) A sixty day furlough with my wife and new baby daughter. (3) A good meal with no bully-beef, and a glass of milk. (4) A plush-lined slit trench. (5) A tile bathroom with hot and cold water, etc. (6) A bed with springs. (7) A haircut by a barber. (8) A front seat for our victory march through Tokyo. (9) One sock (G.I.) at Hitler, Mussy and Hirohito.

Lest you get the wrong impression, we are doing quite nicely with-

The war changed almost everything; it even affected Christmas advertising dramatically. The New York department store Abraham & Straus abandoned the usual Christmas Day ads for holiday sales in favor of photographs of letters sent to the company by employees serving on the front.

out the aforesaid luxuries. We are a happy gang with plenty of fun mixed with our work. Our forces can and will beat those Yellow . . . We all expect to be home by Christmas 194_. We get the good news from Egypt, Russia, Algeria by radio and pray for a continuance of that good news. We gripe about the food, but we get plenty of it—also vitamin pills to round out the menu. I, personally, am in the best of health and spirits. I could well use all the above "gifts" but can do without them until we win this war.

> Regards and good luck
> to you all,
> Stan

Christmas Eve and a Blown Dish Washing Machine

WHEN I LOOKED at the bulletin, I saw my name on a list for kitchen duty on Christmas Eve—from 2 P.M. to midnight.

On Christmas Eve, I was called out into a formation of twenty men and marched to a mess hall. We were turned over to the mess sergeant and the first job he gave me was peeling potatoes. I had never seen such a mountain of potatoes. I said, "I thought you peeled this many potatoes with a machine. That's what we did at the hotel I worked for in Memphis." "Oh, is that so?" asked the mess sergeant. I found out real quick that I was the potato peeling machine at this air base. . . .

There was a dish washing machine with more dirty dishes around it than the machine could possibly wash in a year. I started putting dishes through it, one basket full after another. About 11:30 P.M., it happened. The water supply pipe to the washer blew apart. Water sprayed everywhere, flooding the dish washing room and pouring out into the mess hall.

I looked at the swirling water and just sat down on the floor in it. I sat there thinking, "Boy, this is some Christmas Eve." Lumps came up into my throat. This was the first Christmas I had been away from home. Another soldier working with me ran out, looking for the mess sergeant. I must have sat in the water twenty minutes before the soldier got back with the mess sergeant.

In another few minutes, it was going to be Christmas morning but this sergeant didn't look anything like Santa Claus to me. The sergeant

John Robinson, new recruit at Keesler Air Force Base in Biloxi, Mississippi, in charge of potato peeling on Christmas Eve 1942, encountered more challenges than the potatoes that night. But later, during the course of the war, as a fighter pilot flying with the movie star Jimmy Stewart, Robinson would face and survive even greater challenges.

War bonds—Bob Hope sold them, and so did Bugs Bunny. Waging war on two fronts around the world required an enormous amount of money, and war bonds were a vital means by which the government induced citizens to lend their savings for the war effort. This United States Steel ad in **The Saturday Evening Post** *is a good example of the appeal to parents to invest in their children's future—here by giving a child the ideal Christmas present—by investing in his country. As in World War I, Hollywood also joined the campaign, with star-laden caravans going on multicity tours to stir up interest in bond purchases. Moviegoers heard the appeal at theaters, too, where public-interest short subjects and even cartoons urged people to buy a bond, which could often be done in the theater's lobby.*

☆ ☆ ☆

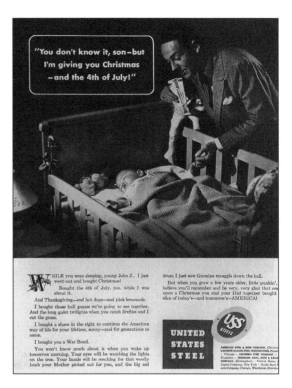

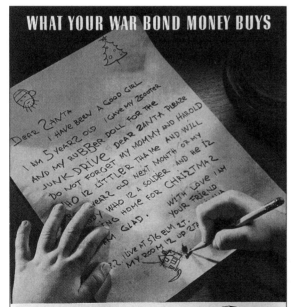

While the sale of war bonds was an important part of the government's strategy for financing the war, it was also a useful means of linking the populace to the war effort. Secretary of the Treasury Henry Morgenthau summed up this angle when he proposed that the government could "use **bonds** *to sell the* **war,** *rather than* **vice versa.***" Hence, the message in this ad, "What Your Bond Money Buys," could also be read as "Why Your Support for the War Effort Is Important." The child's reference in the letter to the scooter and the doll she gave to the "junk drive" refers to the conservation of strategic materials through recycling. It was also a way of enlisting children in the cause. Young people were typically urged to bring their junk to a movie theater or store for collection.*

☆ ☆ ☆

began screaming and looking around. He had no idea where to turn off the water.

I said, "For god's sake, sergeant, get me a pair of pliers. Even a wrench of some kind. I'll fix the damned thing." The sergeant came back with a pair of pliers and a pipe wrench. I said, "Don't worry about it. I'm a hotel engineer. I'll stop the water."

After a few minutes luck was with me and I was able to put the packing nut back together. The water stopped coming from the pipe. I said, "Sergeant, this is temporary. It won't hold forever, but it is okay for now."

I sat back down on the floor in the water. The sergeant said, "Get up soldier. What's your name—" I stood up and quickly said, "Robinson, John H. Serial number 34496440."

That was the way I had been told to do it. I was even proud of myself for remembering my serial number. The sergeant said, "Since you stopped the water, I'm going to let you take off."

This was some Christmas present, I thought. I was supposed to get off at midnight anyway.

The Deliverance of Eddie Rickenbacker

For many Americans during the Christmas of 1942, Eddie Rickenbacker again became a heroic figure. In World War I, this former race-car driver became the ace fighter pilot of the Ninety-fourth Aero Pursuit Squadron and personally downed twenty-six enemy craft, earning himself numerous decorations, including the Medal of Honor. Two decades later, Rickenbacker, now over fifty years old and the president of Eastern Airlines, was again participating in a world war, this time inspecting air bases in the Pacific theater. In October 1942 his B-17 crashed several hundred miles north of Samoa, setting him and his seven men adrift on rubber rafts for twenty-three days. His survival was a dramatic story for Christmas.

ON THE EVE OF Christmas week, Captain Eddie Rickenbacker gave the Nation its Christmas story. He could have kept it for commercial exploitation. Doubtless many syndicates have been bidding for exclusive rights to the recital which Rickenbacker and his companions

Newsweek

DECEMBER 28, 1942   15c

THE MAGAZINE OF NEWS SIGNIFICANCE

Special delivery to Emperor Hirohito: "Merry Xmas." What better way to "send him a message"? World War II popular culture often echoed this lighthearted approach to sometimes deadly business. For example, song lyrics approached the anxiety of going overseas with bravado in lines such as "Goodbye Mama/ I'm Off to Yokohama."

☆ ☆ ☆

brought back from another world. Theirs was a tingling tale to thrill even a generation which is now treated to a daily ration of adventure. Out of the sky eight men dropped into the immense and inhospitable bosom of the Pacific. On three life rafts they kept afloat. With them they had only four oranges, a little water, two fishing lines but no bait. One man died. But, after twenty-three days in those watery wastes, deliverance came from those same skies whence they had come. Here was an epic of thirst and hunger, of storm-lashed seas and burning suns, of suffering and fortitude, of duty and loyalty, which would have titillated millions of stay-at-homes.

But Rickenbacker did not sell his experience. He told it. And, out of his mouth, the explanation quickly dawned on the wondering newspapermen at the War Department. This testimony was a testament. This was no new "story," but an old, old story—the story of the star that guided the shepherds of Bethlehem, the story of the light that came to Paul on the road to Damascus, the story of the Fatherhood of God as well as the brotherhood of man. So a sign appeared unto Rickenbacker and his fellows. It seems that one of the company had brought along his Bible. The men sustained themselves by reading it aloud. On the eighth day tormented by their pangs, they prayed "frankly and humbly." And lo! a seagull came and rested on Rickenbacker's shoulder. It was bait for food, and the starving fliers caught some fish with it.

To Rickenbacker and his comrades the truth had been revealed. It is the truth that such faith as he and they had, and such as Mrs. Rickenbacker kept like a flame at home, will surely bring deliverance. That was the testament of an experience which will plumb the depths of the souls of Americans this Christmas time. Look up for guidance, and it shall come. May the Rickenbacker story be retold from the pulpit, in the camp, and at the hearth as we celebrate the birth of the Prince of Peace through Whom the spirit of man is made indestructible.

"... there has to be a line drawn somewhere."

Millions of American women contributed to the war effort. Red Cross women worked both on the home front and in the field; women worked for the USO (United Service Organizations) in various military theaters; female volunteers served at YMCAs; they worked for the Salvation Army; they worked as nurses; they served in various military units; they worked in shipyards and aircraft factories, and aided the American cause in countless other roles. From "Rosie the Riveters" to switchboard operators, they stepped forward to serve. But in Poughkeepsie, New York, there was one role over Christmas 1942 they did not perform.

Santas To Appear In City Again
Chicago Introduces Lady St. Nicks But Innovation Will Not Be Attempted Here—Yet

THE TIME HAS COME for some one, in the manner of the old New York Sun, to write "there is a Santa Claus"—not for the benefit of a wondering child this year so much, as for the benefit of Santa's helpers who will be appearing soon at toylands. All because out in Chicago a feminine Santa Claus has been introduced as an answer to the shortage of manpower.

But in Poughkeepsie, at least two representative spots yesterday made it clear, Santa will be Santa and no bearded lady this Yuletide, as usual.

Of course, there are arguments in favor of a lady Santa during wartime. Women have been doing just about everything else that a man had done and probably there is little argument against why they couldn't help out St. Nick. But it would be quite a blow to the kids to climb aboard her lap and hear a staccato: "What would you like me to bring you, sonny?" in place of the customary voice of pleasant gruffness.

The fact that a lady St. Nick has made her appearance in Chicago, however, received the same kind of reception here last week as it did in New York where word was that Santa would prevail as usual during the holiday season.

"What next!" exclaimed the head of one of the city's department stores. "If we have a Santa Claus again this year, he will be a man."

"We expect Santa to be here—himself," commented another.

No attempt was made at belittling the forthright efforts that have been put forth during wartime by the feminine populace—but there has to be a line drawn some place.

And Santa Claus seems to be it.

Christmas, Wartime, and a Wedding

DECEMBER 25, 1942, was, and always will be, the most memorable Christmas to me because it was also my wedding day.

My fiancé, Harold, was in the military service; he was stationed in Long Beach, California, and I had come out from Denver to visit him in November. We decided to marry as soon as possible.

I got a job with Western Union, rented a small apartment in Los Angeles—and waited for the only dates Harold could get leave: late Christmas Eve and Christmas Day. My mother sent me a pretty bridesmaid dress I had once worn—that was my makeshift wedding gown. I bought a gardenia from a street vendor to carry as my bouquet.

When Western Union finally closed at midnight on Christmas Eve, I rushed home to pick up my dress, then dashed for the streetcar to take me to the church—where Harold was pacing nervously back and forth, waiting. Within a few minutes of arrival, I'd changed into my dress and was walking down the aisle on the arm of an old friend of my parents. Harold and I spoke our vows at 1:30 A.M. in front of ready-made but unknown guests—a full congregation who had just heard the benediction to a traditional Christmas Eve ceremony. How startled they must have been to hear the wedding march follow a Christmas carol! Afterward, a kind young couple—again, strangers—used their precious rationed gas to drive us back to the apartment. Our wedding may have been "rushed," but our marriage hasn't been—it's lasted 51 years!

For Esther Carlson, the Christmas of 1942 had special meaning. Like many young couples faced with the conflicting emotional pressures of love, war, and the immediate prospect of separation, the two decided to marry during a fleeting time together—at Christmastime.

This is no ordinary junior high, where the students are preparing their Christmas cards. It's at a relocation camp in Colorado for Japanese-Americans. After Pearl Harbor, fear grew that Americans of Japanese descent might undermine the war effort by siding with their ancestral homeland, even though no pattern of disloyalty among them was ever discovered.

✯ ✯ ✯

A Christmas Feast
for an Ambulance Driver

In 1914 Joseph Desloge had volunteered as a driver of Ford Model T ambulances with the French in World War I. After the Japanese attacked Pearl Harbor in December 1941, Desloge encouraged his sixteen-year-old son, Joseph Desloge, Jr., to sign up with the American Field Service as an ambulance driver for the British troops in North Africa. Throughout the war, Desloge sent long letters to his father. His friends and relatives in the States nicknamed him "the Ernie Pyle of the British Army."

MY FIRST CHRISTMAS AWAY from home was the most memorable of the war. The Battle of El Alamein had been won, and we were sitting in the desert with the Germans now far to the west. With great willpower I saved all my packages from home for Christmas Day; I didn't open a single one. On The Day I opened Papa's first. He had sent me sheet music for some folk tunes, which I proceeded to practice on my banjo right away, with time out for great helpings of cookies and fruit cake. Pretty soon I was stuffed; I thought I would burst. Only one small package remained to be opened, and it turned out to be a tin of chewing tobacco, which my friend Martin Lammert sent me. He must have thought it would be the appropriate thing to send to someone serving with the notorious French Foreign Legion. I sampled it. "Pretty good," I thought. Unfortunately no one told me not to swallow the juice. I became sick as a dog and threw up all the goodies I had been saving for so long. The only thing retrievable was my sheet music!

This 1942 Christmas ad in **The Saturday Evening Post** *for the Women's Army Auxiliary Corps, reflecting its times, views women as perhaps too frivolous for serious things and needing a gender-specific sense of satisfaction from their work: "You wouldn't trade that proud feeling for a mink coat and a bushel of orchids!"*

The WAAC came into existence in May 1941 to free Army men from jobs such as clerk, messenger, and lab assistant. Initially, the military objected strongly to having women shatter its male culture, so in a compromise, it was agreed that the WAAC would work **with,** *but not* **in** *the Army. But by July 1943, the Army needed more help overseas. Women would have to be* **in** *the Army to receive full military benefits, so the "Auxiliary" was dropped and the members of the new Women's Army Corps, or WAC, became enlistees.*

★ ★ ★

*For the Fazio family in New York City, the Christmas present from one of their four sons in the service has arrived in January, but is no less cherished because it's a bit late. The family proudly displays a symbol of their boys' service to their country—a flag with four blue stars hangs in the background. Many families had more than one son far away during World War II (the Roosevelts had four), but for one family, that separation turned into a loss of immeasurable magnitude. The five Sullivan brothers of Waterloo, Iowa, enlisted in the Navy when a friend of theirs was killed at Pearl Harbor. At their fateful request, they served together, and on November 14, 1942, died together when their ship, the USS **Juneau,** was sunk in the battle for Guadalcanal. In their memory a destroyer was christened the USS **The Sullivans.** The last of the Sullivan children, a girl, honored her brothers in a way they would have understood. She joined the Navy and became a WAVE, the Women's Reserve of the U.S. Naval Reserve.*

✫ ✫ ✫

A Message from the First Lady

Like no other first lady before her, Eleanor Roosevelt was a towering presence in the country's national life. From her charitable work to her efforts in human rights, she labored tirelessly for numerous causes. Her newspaper columns in papers across the country made friends of millions of readers. When she spoke of the ache of loneliness and the burdens of sacrifice over the Christmas of 1942, many people felt a deeper sense of community. She later wrote: "If human beings can be trained for cruelty and greed and belief in power which comes through hate and fear and

force, certainly we can train equally well for gentleness and mercy and the power of love which comes because of the strength of the good qualities to be found in the soul of every individual human being."

How completely the character of Christmas has changed this year. I could no more say to you: "A Merry Christmas" without feeling a catch in my throat than I could fly to the moon! We all know that for too many people this will be anything but a Merry Christmas. It can, however, be a Christmas Season of deep meaning to us all.

Remembering the Father Who Wrote "White Christmas"

In 1941 Irving Berlin was asked to write songs about the major holidays of the year for a 1942 movie called **Holiday Inn,** *starring Bing Crosby and Fred Astaire. On Christmas Day 1941, Crosby introduced Berlin's "White Christmas" on* **The Kraft Music Hall.** *It was an instant sensation and became the biggest-selling single of all time. During the war Crosby and Berlin both toured battle areas and "White Christmas" was one of the favorite songs of the troops. In 1942 Mary Ellin, Berlin's daughter, was sixteen years old. Visiting her father, who was on tour in Detroit at Christmastime, she was caught in the media frenzy accorded a celebrity.*

There was a flurry of excitement, Christmas of 1942, when my mother, sisters, and I, our war-time priorities clutched in our hands, boarded the train, crowded with "cute" servicemen ("Keep moving, dear, no talking to strangers, dear - . . . dear"), to meet our touring father in Detroit. A few more days of being in the thick of things. A photographer snapping us in our suite at the Book-Cadillac, with our hotel Christmas tree, for next year's card, my mother said, but also for the Detroit papers, permissible publicity considering the cause . . .

And everywhere I went they'd be playing— as if *This Is the Army* weren't enough—the country's number one tune, "White Christmas," not only the instant property of homesick servicemen across the seas, but a song boys and girls on the home front danced to, fell in love to, adopted as "their" song. ☆

The Christmas Story is a reminder to us of a life so unselfish, so completely lived in the interests of other people that there was no room in it anywhere for thought of self. Christ knew that at the end of His life He would have to pay the supreme sacrifice, and yet He was willing to make that sacrifice in order that life might have a little more meaning and a little more hope for His brothers and sisters in the world of His day and forever thereafter.

Many of the young people today are doing their jobs in the present world crisis with exactly the same hope in their hearts, and it is this spirit of divine sacrifice and love for your fellow human beings which gives to the Christmas Season its real spiritual significance.

Whatever our particular religious beliefs may be, we still can feel a share in this Christmas spirit and try to do our part at this Season by making life just a little bit brighter wherever we touch it. So many families will be divided, so many people will find their hearts hovering over far away places, that it will be hard even to keep "a smiling face" as Robert Louis Stevenson admonished us to do.

You will perhaps remember the story of the man who had nothing in the world to give and so he always gave a smile, and when he reached St. Peter's gate, the little Angels that welcomed him in were the happy thoughts that he had inspired by his smile.

I am going as usual on Christmas morning to a church service and then I hope to have time for a flying visit to Walter Reed Hospital to the wards where some of our returned wounded from Africa are being treated. After that I will stop for a few minutes at the YWCA where they are having a Christmas dinner for Government workers who are strangers in Washington and who have no family connections here. This seems to me a very nice gesture for the YWCA to make, and I am glad to be given the opportunity to stop in for a few minutes to wish them all a pleasant day, before returning to our own family concerns for the rest of the day.

E.R.

☆ ☆ ☆

V meant at least two important things to American servicemen. It stood, of course, for their ultimate goal, victory. But for the GIs, V also stood for something more mundane, something they looked forward to every week: V-Mail.

Dearest Jodie Boy:

Well, just back from Long Cave, after a most delightful day. Went up with Jan. Reg and Bobbie brought me back. There was a lovely dinner (basket lunch) at the Long Cave Methodist Church, served in the "Hut."—Baked chicken, fried chicken, country ham, dressing, salads, cakes, everything else you can think of and want. Pretty tree and gifts for everyone. Can you imagine it, I got a large box of roasted pecans—Just save me the trouble of picking some out—Wish you had them.

You should see what I brought home, backbone and spare ribs, sausage, liver pudding, butter and turnip salad (doesn't that sound natural?)—Oh, yes, I almost forgot my Christmas presents—two nice gowns, a Jergen toilet set, lovely toilet soap, wash rags and candy—So Santa Claus came early this year. Everything useful as well as nice. The gifts were from all the folks . . .

Know you did appreciate and enjoy your Christmas box from the "Jaycees." Think it was lovely of them to remember you. Bet they bought [it] at Neal-Shaefers. One day recently, Steve hinted that some one was sending you a nice toilet set. Hope you have gotten my boxes, at least two of them by now . . . Guess you will have enough candy for once, but just tuck some of it away to enjoy after Christmas is gone if you can. You had better save some of these boxes to send some of those things home that you cannot take care of out there. Course keep all you need and want.

Well, Honey guess this about is all the news for this time, will write you again soon. Hoping you will have a nice Xmas. Mother will be thinking of you, and wishing you the best of everything. Enjoy the football game and remember every man in this town would like to be right there with you. All the folks send love and best wishes for Merry Christmas.

With lots of love. Again best wishes for a nice Christmas.
Lots of love,
Mother.

In April 1942, after enlisting in the "SeaBees," the Navy's construction battalions, Joseph Barrow of West Point, Georgia, trained at Norfolk and was sent to the West Coast. From these early days of his war service to his time in war zones of the western Pacific, Barrow was kept abreast of the occurrences on the home front by his mother, Margaret Barrow. As she made clear, the whole town was his family.

Books such as **So Your Husband's Gone to War!** and **The Navy Wife,** displayed here in a Macy's window, made appropriate and useful Christmas presents in 1942. The difficulty of running a household with appliances almost impossible to find and so many necessities, such as meat, rationed, was often over-shadowed by anxiety about how to cope with the absence of a husband. About 8 percent of the 50 million adult women in the country would have husbands in the military by 1945. But twice that many saw their sons off to war.

☆ ☆ ☆

Prayer of a Jewish Sergeant at Christmas

Although they were not intended to be a melting pot, the Armed Forces during World War II brought together men of different religions and ethnic backgrounds who might have had little social contact with each other in civilian life. It put these men not only in close quarters for extended periods of time, but also in situations where they totally depended on one another—often for their very lives. Movies of the period reflected this mix, with platoons of men with names such as Cohen, Kelly, Sanchez, and Gabriloviwcz. Slightly more than half a *million of these World War II soldiers were Jews, probably more than half of them first-generation Americans. Eighty percent were in the Army. In this letter to his family, Sergeant Sanford Cohen describes how Christmas Day 1942 made those differences look a bit less significant when circumstances required cooperation, understanding, friendship, and goodwill.*

December 26, 1942

Dear Mother, Dad and Family:

My last letter to you was just about a week ago, but I have a few interesting things to tell you. . . . I want to describe to you the scene in my tent just two nights ago, Christmas Eve. First, I want you to understand that there are five Jewish boys and two Catholic fellows, in the tent. Three Jewish fellows from New York, including myself (Bronx, Brooklyn and Manhattan), one from Chicago and one from Texas, and one Catholic from Texas, the other from Wisconsin. This last boy has great admiration and respect for me, I believe because of my seniority in age, and would do anything in the world for me. So, in keeping with the principles of Americanism, we helped them celebrate their holiday. On a particular evening, we were all lying on our bunks resting from the day's work and talking together. At 8:30, I called the boys around the fire and held a brief service. I read them a little prayer that I had written especially that morning. This is what I wrote:

> *Our Father in Heaven, as we, thy children, sit before Thee on this holy night, we offer our humble thanks! Though we are many miles from our homes and our loved ones, there are many things to be thankful for. We thank Thee for bringing us into this strange land in safety and for being with us and giving us spirit. We thank Thee for keeping us strong in body, strong in mind, and free from harm. We thank Thee for giving us shelter to cover our heads, and food to satisfy our hunger. And we pray that Thou continue to watch over us and guide us on this treacherous path in our lives.*
>
> *But more than we ask for ourselves, we beseech Thee to bring Thy blessing to our dear parents, to our families and to our loved*

ones. Bring peace and happiness into their homes and keep them well. Give them great strength and fortitude that they may carry on through these trying times with their heads held high. Cause them not to worry nor to have anxiety toward us, and relieve their troubled minds by bringing them our awaited letters as regularly as possible.

And now, we ask that Thou give Thy blessing to our cause, and in the name of humanity, make us victorious. And then, when our task is done and our goal accomplished, we pray that Thou return us safely to our native land, to our homes, to our families and friends. May peace, tranquility and tolerance reign over all the earth forevermore. Amen.

Then all the boys stood up, and I said a few Hebrew words from the Sabbath benediction, translating into English. This was followed by the singing of the Lord's Prayer by the Wisconsin boy and myself, and then everybody joined in for a few carols. Then we scrambled up our eggs and, special for the occasion, we mixed in some canned corned beef that I had been saving. And with the delicious eating thereof, so ended Christmas Eve!

On Christmas Day, we worked for a change! But here's the good part. The pilot who flies my ship likes me a lot and sent up some cake and candy to my tent as a little present. In return we invited him up to the tent to have eggs with us in the evening. He came up and we had a great time together. He sure is a swell fellow. . . .

☆ ☆ ☆
These sailors are holding Christmas gift boxes, given to them by the people of Puerto Rico—and there are plenty more boxes behind them. While no fighting took place in Puerto Rico in World War II, American strategists early on saw its strategic importance as a base of operations for the defense of the Caribbean and the South Atlantic.

53

Christmas Dinner
with the Queen Mother

For Captain Charles L. Badley of Berkeley, California, Christmas in Britain in 1942 would be memorable, for he celebrated it in royal style, at dinner with the Queen Mother, the grandmother of Queen Elizabeth II. The British Royal Family had begun to build important ties to America in 1939 when George VI became the first British monarch to visit the United States. He and his wife, Elizabeth, were hosted by President and Mrs. Roosevelt and treated to an informal hot dog lunch—the guests were delighted—as well as state dinners. Captain Badley's host, Queen Mary, was the mother of George VI and wife of King George V, who had died in 1936. The queen was somewhat shy in public, but, as Badley's account makes clear, informal and friendly in private, and a warm host at Christmastime to several representative American servicemen. The captain's letter is addressed to his colleagues at the office at his peacetime job back at the Celotex Corporation, as well as to his mother.

December 30, 1942

DEAR MOTHER, DAD AND GANG: Though I can't tell you exactly where I was, or the mission engaged upon, or the military impediments of the moment, I think even the hardest of censors would let a guy tell you just a bit about Christmas Day as I enjoyed it over here. I must, of course, start with Christmas Eve. 'Twas then that I opened the various Christmas parcels which had been arriving for two weeks or more before Christmas. Piled beneath my cot they began to assume more importance than .30 calibre ammunition to an isolated Infantry company in combat. They soon became the talk of the other officers who (the greedy little brutes) had crawled away to dark corners when their packages had arrived and opened them in places far from the rest of us where there was little danger of mass appropriation. There in the room before me as I entered were all my officers, grouped like a tribunal council, sitting in a semi-circle around my cot on their haunches. I could have charged them with violations of every article of war, and the Constitution to boot, and they wouldn't have budged. Together we opened my Christmas packages. The guard on the post outside was given instructions to admit no one, not even Eisenhower, himself, if he, too, should attempt to crash my Christmas party; the blackouts adjusted, and the session began.

Dad will remember Christmas on Cebu Island, some forty-odd years ago, and can add that part of the tale I can't describe. It's about the way a guy feels when the holidays roll around, and it hits him with a jolt that the home folks and the old gang and the Statue of Liberty are thousands of miles, and a war and a victory away, and the going a bit rough in spots, and there are strangers everywhere—and it's Christmas Eve.

The two packages from home were opened first. The TollHouse

With Christmas coming on, the crew members of the submarine USS **Dolphin** *pass mail down below as one member stops to read a letter above. The* **Dolphin** *was built at the Portsmouth Naval Shipyard and launched in 1932. Its home port was Pearl Harbor, and on the morning of December 7, 1941, it brought down one of the attacking Japanese planes with its deck gun. The* **Dolphin** *was awarded two battle stars during World War II—for action at Pearl Harbor and in the 1942 Battle of Midway. The USS* **Dolphin** *was decommissioned after the war.*

★ ★ ★

cookies, Mother, were immediately spread out ('twas the suggestion of my Senior First Lieutenant, the rat). Throughout the evening those conscienceless hounds made similarly generous suggestions through mouths stuffed full. . . . To each and all of you my heartfelt gratitude.

What a social whirl I had during the next two days, ending with the event to end all events, dinner on Christmas Day with Queen Mary!

Due to your generosity, it was possible for me to go to each home with a package for the host or hostess or perhaps her charming daughter, neatly wrapped in re-used holly paper and bright string, and containing a bar of soap, or a few packets of American cigarettes, or some candy, or a packet or two of razor blades. All items that can't be gotten over here are more appreciated here, I am sure, than you folks can begin to imagine.

At last my dinner engagement at the Queen Mother's. Nearly all of you contributed with one thing or another to the gift package I carted along to be presented to Her Majesty. Lieutenant Brush, who accompanied me as the only other American guest present, thought I was a bit crazy, but I felt all along I knew what I was about. Met in the royal hall by a doorman, so to speak, whose quiet dignity and poise made me feel a bit like an unshod hillbilly in town for the very first time. I was helped off with my coat, clutching the while the unwrapped parcel which bore on its outside the rather unfestive statement: "Perfection Paper Clips-6 gross." Asked if this were a gift for Her Majesty, I replied in the affirmative and found myself ushered along through the next wide portals to a larger hall where I was met by Lord Claud Hamilton who received me and Lt. Brush most cordially. He asked if my package contained a gift for Her Majesty, and he graciously took it from me when I replied yes and said he would give me an opportunity to present it later. Lord Claud conducted us through another and wider portal

56

Private First Class Richard Balzarini, a marine stationed in Iceland, received a bittersweet Christmas package from his hometown of East Natick, Massachusetts. It was from his brother, Frank. Several weeks before, on November 28, 1942, Frank, a headwaiter at the Coconut Grove nightclub in Boston, had died attempting to save the lives of some of those trapped in a horrendous-blazing fire. Nearly five hundred people lost their lives that night, the worst fire disaster in United States history. Ironically, in the package Frank had mailed before his death, he enclosed several photographs of the club. Richard had learned of the tragedy in a short cablegram: "Frank gave his life saving others. Please be brave. Details later. Mother."

☆ ☆ ☆

into the Queen's parlor where the guests of the evening were assembled. Lovely people and everyone titled except the five military people present—we two Americans and three British officers. Immediately following the introductions Queen Mary entered the room to the curtsies of the ladies present and the bows of the gentlemen. She greeted each of us individually, giving us her hand and looking the while as sweet and lovely as a sixteen-year-old girl. Having thus greeted her guests, she came over to me and Lt. Brush, excused herself from the other guests and requested us to follow her into her sitting room. As I passed through the door into this room Lord Claud placed my package in my hands and the next moment Sam Brush, Her Majesty, and I were together, I again holding the paper-clip box in what I shall ever hope was a nonchalant and born-to-the-purple manner. She put us completely at ease immediately, telling us how happy she was to have us there and also to say she hoped we would accept a little Christmas gift from her.

Whereupon she took from a table two packages and was about to hand them to us when she observed the rude cardboard box in my hands. She sweetly asked me if, perchance, that could be a gift for her. Vainly trying to hide the paper clip label, I nonchalantly placed the

Merchant seamen hold candy-filled boots they have won at a Christmas party in New York City. It was small compensation for the role they filled in World War II. Each American soldier in the field required seven to fifteen tons of supplies per year, and getting it to them was the job of men like these seamen. About 7,000 merchant seamen were killed in action in the war, giving them the worst mortality rate of all the services.

★ ★ ★

box on a table behind me and mumbled somethin about it being rather nothing at all—just a little potpourri from America that I had whipped together from parcels from the folks and gang back home and thought perhaps she might be interested in glancing through some time at her leisure—then, turning, perhaps too eagerly to accept my gift. It was graciously handed over, opened, and, to my joy it was a beautiful cigarette case of silver, engraved with her initials and the royal coat of arms or her crest, I believe. Lieutenant Brush received a set consisting of a silver pen knife and silver pencil, likewise engraved. Our heartfelt thanks were given, and then, while all the guests awaited in the other room the Queen Mother undid the paper clip box and eagerly went through the package. She seemed pleased no end, thanked me most graciously, had one of her staff come in immediately to take my gift and have it displayed in the other room along with the jewels and priceless antiques she had received as Christmas gifts. We rejoined the guests then, chatted for a few minutes and then went on, in proper order to the dining room. Lord Claud had come to me just before we left for the dining hall to advise that I was to sit at the Queen's left and Captain Thornelee of the British Army on her right. He and I followed Her Majesty into the dining hall, found our proper places, and as smoothly as a well-rehearsed movie scene, were all seated and the dinner was under way . . .

During dinner most of my conversation was with Queen Mary. We discussed America and Canada and England.

You will recall the favors we used to distribute at parties when we were kids. The cardboard tubes with paper tassels at the ends that we would pull causing a loud explosion. Inside was a motto, or a fortune, some sort of gift, and always a paper hat. These the English call "crackers" and a very fancy type of these were distributed during the last course of the dinner. When all were distributed, each guest crossed his arms, taking the end of the "cracker" of the guest on either side. A pause, then, that each could make a wish that was bound to come true and then all together the crackers were exploded. Great laughter and much fun all around the table as the favors were opened and we found our mottoes, our tiny gifts and our paper hats. These were promptly put on and I wondered what the War Department would have done to this Captain to see him sitting along-side the Queen Mother with a pink hat that bloomed out above my khaki in tassels and frills! The fact that the Queen wore a similar headpiece might have helped.

The Queen was interested in my stories of our Christmases at home. We spent some little time, Mother, talking of you. The Queen told me how she wished it were possible for you to have been there and asked me if I would be so kind as to send along a little gift from her to you. On the table were some velvet roses which her Majesty told me were used annually for decorations on the table at Christmas time. She gave me one of these to send to you, Mother, and I will mail this along.

When Lieutenant Brush and I left at midnight it was with the feeling that we had been all evening with old and dear friends. Everything had been sincere hospitality, gratefully received. Nothing had been strained or false or patronizing. It was grand. Must close for tonight. Hope you are all well, happy and that all goes well.

Love,
Charlie

★ ★ ★

By Christmas 1942, the American public, having been warned about the potential danger of enemy planes, would have quickly picked up on the humor in seeing Santa tracked with an antiaircraft light.

This cover of **Homefront** *magazine for its issue at Christmas 1942, one year into America's participation in World War II, makes dramatically clear what the conflict meant to Americans. GIs, far away from everything and everyone they love and care about, try to warm their hands over the fire outside their tent, while their thoughts and feelings are warmed by memories of home here depicted as a snowy New England village on Christmas Eve.* **Homefront** *was unique in these momentous years, a nonprofit publication published from 1942 to 1946 by J. Horace and Monica L. Strunk of Bangor, Pennsylvania, for hometown GIs serving overseas. Its pages were filled with news and photos from home, including the latest on Bangor's servicemen and -women. Amid its messages of hope and inspiration each month was also a photograph of the "Fairest of the Month," a tasteful picture of a local young woman that invariably served as a pinup in barracks and tents in Europe, North Africa, and throughout the Pacific.*

✫ ✫ ✫

Chaplain's Message from Homefront

 Any priest or minister has a problem at Christmas: How to remind the flock that amid the distractions of holiday shopping, putting up and trimming the tree, writing the cards, cleaning the house for visitors, cooking and general merrymaking, there is a transcendent reason for all

of it that overshadows the minutiae of preparation and celebration. At the heart of it all is the story of a birth long ago and its meaning and message for the world. Without that meaning and that message, it would be just another day off from school and work. Chaplain First Lieutenant Archie C. Rohrbaugh has the additional difficulty of bringing home that message to men who are far from home this Christmas 1942 and who have greater and graver distractions. Here the Chaplain reminds them that the one brighter star in the firmament at Christmas shines in the night sky just as strongly when it's visible through the flaps of a tent as when it may be seen through the living-room window.

CHRISTMAS! The very word suggests much. It conjures up in our minds pleasant days at home with decorated Christmas trees, a table heavy with roast and trimmings, and lively conversation with all the family present. It suggests coziness, comfort, and enjoyable moments.

But Christmas means more to us than that. It conveys a deeper, more solemn note. With its music, beautiful carols and great cantatas sung in our churches or heard on the radio, it thrills our souls. Its recitations and pageantry in our Sunday schools bring back memories of days when we said our "pieces" and remind us that soon our footprints will be all that remain in the sands of time, and that this mortal flesh will be no more. With its harmony of music, word, and spirit it sobers us and sends us into the crisp winter air feeling better, resolved to live as man should in God's wonderful world.

Christmas means even more. Behind its enjoyable moments lies the most glorious realization that Christ was born. It brings to us the fact that the Child of God was born into the world, and that by His light the darkness of the earth would some day be dispelled, and the people live in peace and joy as people should. Christmas is the Child in the manger, the star overhead, the angels singing to the shepherds, and the Wise Men coming to worship Him. This is the true meaning of Christmas and once a man has seen it in all its glory he is never the same afterward. Forever, in his heart, there will be a manger, and, cradled there, the Christ Child.

On this Christmas many of us will not be home. The only carols we may hear will be those sung among ourselves, with a lone chaplain in our midst, by the side of our guns. It may be a heart-rending Christmas as we think of the folk at home. It certainly will not be as we were accustomed to having it, yet, somehow, we will gladly endure it.

Away from home, in camp or on battlefield, we will have a grand privilege. We will be able to see the stars at night as we look up from our guns. They will be beautiful stars. And, when we look, like the wise men we may be able to see one brighter than all the rest. And, if we listen, like the shepherds, we may be able to hear angel voices in the whispering breeze. Ours will be the privilege of seeing the Christ-child as he was first seen from open field and desert. We, too, can have a manger with a Christ-child in it. Yes, if only we will, wherever we are we can have Mary the Mother, the Child, the manger, the shepherds, angels, and wise men. For, no man can possess these things except he hold them in his heart.

*Cadets at the Army's separate flying school for black pilots study their craft at Tuskegee, Alabama, just after Christmas 1942, two months before the first class graduated. Tuskegee trained 1,300 men during the war, and 450, known as the Tuskegee Airmen, saw action over North Africa, Sicily, and other European theaters. The group that the Germans respectfully dubbed the **Schwartze Vogelmenschen** ("Black Birdmen") was led by Colonel Benjamin O. Davis, later the Air Force's first black general. They flew 1,578 missions, the first of them in June 1943. The Tuskegee Airmen were subjected to constant carping from white officers about their alleged lack of effectiveness—not proved—and in 1945, in Indiana, some of them were court-martialed for refusing to accept the segregation of an officers' club.*

★ ★ ★

The music of Irving Berlin and performances by Bing Crosby (left) and Fred Astaire (above, from left, Crosby, Marjorie Reynolds, Astaire, and Virginia Dale) made the film **Holiday Inn** successful as America passed through its first full year of war. The movie's plot follows a performer who retires to Connecticut, only to still feel the pull of show business. The solution: operate an inn that's open only for the holidays. The songs from the film included "Be Careful, It's My Heart," "Happy Holidays," and the now perennial and quintessential Christmas song "White Christmas," sung by Crosby, winner of the Oscar for Best Song in 1944.

★ ★ ★

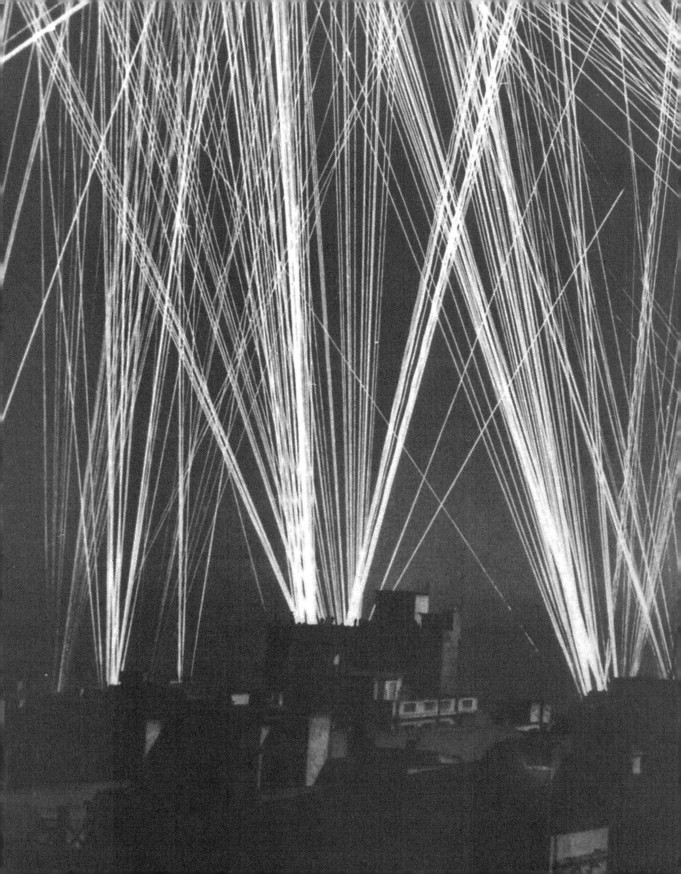

1943

★ ★ ★

THE WAR had become a test of endurance and will. Early in 1943, President Roosevelt and Prime Minister Churchill, meeting in Casablanca, Morocco, announced that the unconditional surrender of the Axis powers would be the only acceptable basis for ending the war. Later, Roosevelt declared in a radio speech, "In our uncompromising policy, we mean no harm to the common people of the Axis nations. But we do mean to impose punishment and retribution in full upon their guilty, barbaric leaders."

Axis forces suffered major defeats in 1943. In North Africa in the spring, with U.S. forces attacking from the west and the British from the east, Axis troops were driven into retreat and more than 200,000 were captured.

Despite enduring staggering human losses, the Soviets announced in 1943 that they had broken the Nazi siege of Leningrad, a terrible ordeal that had lasted since the early days of the war. German soldiers, dispirited and suffering in the frigid cold, their equipment and supply lines cut off, limped eastward back to their homeland. Hitler's awesome firepower on the Russian front had died in the snowbanks and winds. In early September, British and Canadian troops invaded Italy from Sicily. Five days later the Italians surrendered unconditionally.

On the home front in America, weary citizens watched Gary Cooper and Ingrid Bergman's movie version of Hemingway's *For Whom the Bell Tolls* and also the first Lassie film, *Lassie Come Home,* which premiered in October and starred Roddy McDowall, Donald Crisp, Dame Mae Whitty, and Elizabeth Taylor. They bought 78 rpm records of the Andrews Sisters singing "Pistol Packin' Mama" and, in time for the Christmas season, "Jingle Bells."

On Christmas Eve, the third since the war had begun for the United States, President Roosevelt appointed General Eisenhower supreme commander of Allied forces. His mission: to coordinate "Operation Overlord," a plan to invade Europe and bring down, in total defeat, the German army.

This cartoon, from the front page of **The Washington Evening Star,** *depicts one of the rare times that Uncle Sam has ever been shown kneeling. That fact alone indicates just how strongly Americans felt about their boys who had to spend Christmas far from home, possibly in harm's way. The use of the image of Uncle Sam to symbolize the United States had been widespread since the nineteenth century, most prominently on the World War I and II selective service poster, in which he points at the viewer and says, "I want* **you.***"*

★ ★ ★

On a Texas Air Force Base—
A Woman Pilot Trainee and the Enemy

From all over the United States, women who had learned to fly gave up jobs, left home, and traveled to Air Force camps, most of them in Texas. They were part of the Women Airforce Service Pilots (WASP), and Hazel Hohn was one of them. At Avenger Field, the site of the Texas State Technical College at Sweetwater today, Hazel and her mates tolerated the dust and heat and did what they loved to do the most—fly planes. They trained for possible military action that never came. On Christmas Day 1943, Hazel Hohn left Avenger Field for a short trip and met some men she would never forget.

IT WAS CHRISTMAS 1943, and all five of us in our bay were far from home. We were women Air Force pilot trainees at Avenger Field, in Texas, and had nearly finished primary training. Everyone in our bay but me had received her Christmas package from home.

It looked as though I would have nothing to open on Christmas morning for the first time in my life. But one of my baymates went to the PX and bought me a small bottle of cologne, so I would not be left out. Her kind gesture made my day.

That afternoon, we went in different directions. Two other pilot trainees and I had been invited by a chaplain to the Army base in Abilene, Texas, to have Christmas dinner and spend the afternoon with soldiers stationed there. After two months at an all-female air base, we looked forward to that.

When we arrived in Abilene, a 50-mile drive, we were driven to the base and met by our soldier hosts. Going into the base, we noticed the festive Christmas decorations on all the barracks except one, which had very sparse decorations and was surrounded by mud, with wooden planks laid across to walk on.

★ ★ ★
John Maloney crystalized the hopes of the world in this 1943 cartoon.

We waste not the Meat

Waste not the food of war. With proud and thankful hearts let's give our fighters the meat to fight on

This year a lot of boys are spending their holidays in faraway lands. This time a lot of boys will be eating Christmas dinner from a mess kit.

Lest we forget, the ounce of meat we save is an ounce of insurance that our meat is being used more effectively as a weapon of war.

Among all foods, meat may well be regarded by meal planners as "*the yardstick of protein foods*" because of the high nutritional values which it brings to the table: complete, high-quality proteins, essential B vitamins (thiamine, riboflavin, niacin) and important minerals (iron, copper, phosphorus).

That's why women are learning to prepare with new glamour the cuts available from day to day, all of which contain the same nutritional essentials—every cut of which has its own distinctive flavor.

That's why all of us are learning to relish every single bit of meat . . . every last drop of that good meat gravy.

These nutritional essentials (proteins, B vitamins, minerals) are not stored in the body to any appreciable extent—must be supplied in the daily foods we eat.

ACCEPTED AMERICAN MEDICAL ASSN.

THIS SEAL *means that all nutritional statements made in this ad written on are accepted in the Council on Foods and Nutrition of the American Medical Association.*

AMERICAN MEAT INSTITUTE . . . Chicago

*The cover of **Life** magazine containing this ad had a picture of a pilot's wife leaning out a window. The previous Christmas cover depicted a "lonely wife." They were making a sacrifice, and everyone else on the home front was called upon to do without as well. Meat, cars, gasoline, bicycles, canned goods, sugar, coffee, fuel, oil, and shoes were all being carefully allocated, or else were not available at all.*

✯ ✯ ✯

We wondered why it was so bleak in comparison with the others.

"That's the German POW barracks," an officer told us. "They will be waiting on tables during dinner. But you are strictly forbidden to speak to them or fraternize with them in any way."

Of course we knew that when a superior officer gave us an order, the only possible response was "yes, sir," "no, sir," or "no excuse, sir." We had learned that at the beginning of our induction.

We enjoyed the turkey dinner, sitting at long tables in the mess hall with other soldiers, our hosts, and the chaplain. The POWs served us in silence, and we paid them no attention.

But this bothered one of my fellow pilots, and she discussed it with me. We knew how we felt to be this far from our families and home states, even though we were enjoying the hospitality of others. How much worse it must be for these young men thousands of miles from their home country and loved ones, serving their "enemy" on Christmas Day.

She also felt that since we would still have to coexist with them after the war, it would be better to be friendly now, to let them know that most Americans really wanted peace.

I agreed with her. We knew the penalty for disobeying an order, but this was Christmas, and we felt there was a higher order in effect for this special day.

We got up and went over to some POWs and wished them a Merry Christmas. We did not know if they understood English, but they knew our meaning and wished us Frohliche Weihnachten in return.

Either no one noticed or our superiors chose to ignore our brief "fraternizing."

It was a small gesture, like the bottle of cologne I was given that morning, but it warmed our spirits, and we hoped it did theirs.

As we left to go home, dusk was falling. The POW barracks seemed bleaker than ever in the fading light, with its sea of mud. An officer told us they were having their own Christmas celebration and turkey dinner. As we passed their building, we heard the beautiful sound of Christmas caroling.

Into Harbor at Christmas

IN THE TWO MONTHS PRIOR to Christmas of 1943, the USS *New Orleans* had been at sea almost continuously, striking at the enemy. The men were beginning to expect that their celebration of Christmas would be far from friendly shores and in the midst of hostile action. Imagine their happiness when just two weeks before Christmas, the ship came into harbor—a harbor far from home, but one where Christmas was known and celebrated.

As chaplain of the ship, I began at once to make what arrangements I could for the worship and celebration. Having a Christmas tree was almost too much to be expected, but again Commander S. R. Hickey, with his Fleet Recreation and Morale Office, came through with a tree. It was a real cedar, one among a very few which had come thousands of miles by ship from the good old U.S.A.

A great crowd of the men gathered around when we brought it aboard, staring at it unbelievingly and, too, with wistful looks in their eyes. I sent my able yeoman and right-hand man, Eugene Adams of San Francisco, California, to find what decorations he could, and was greatly surprised when he showed up with the whole works—lights, tinsel and ornaments. We decided the best place to set the tree up would be in the hangar amidship, where divine services, movies and entertainments are held.

Everyone wanted to help, but I gave the job to those ever helpful men, the Master-at-Arms force. Chief Master-at-Arms William Hays of Winchester, Kentucky, another right-hand man to the chaplain, took charge of setting up the tree, assisted by Stewart Brunson of San Diego, California, and Kenneth Gordon Samson of Yakima, Washington. With the seven-foot tree up, Raymond R. Resch of San Diego and "Tony" Cresci of San Francisco strung the lights. Then Otto Gottschim of Huntly, Wyoming, took over the draping of ornaments, assisted by a great, eager crowd of men. Soon we had as beautiful a Christmas tree as could be found anywhere at home.

*The USS **New Orleans** was in Pearl Harbor on December 7, 1941. She survived. The 10,000-ton heavy cruiser later saw action in many of the major naval engagements of the war, from the Battle of the Coral Sea to Guadalcanal. Shortly after a Christmas party held aboard ship in 1943, Chaplain L. Clyde Carter wrote a description of the event and mimeographed copies for the crew.*

★ **1943** ★

This was two days before Christmas Eve. Yet, there was something wrong with our tree—of course, it needed a pile of gifts around it. What to do? I called in our Supply Officer, Commander R. H. Burgess of Flint, Michigan, and he gave us cigarettes and "pogy-bait" (candy) enough for all hands, with the promise of "gedunk" (ice cream) for all hands after our Christmas Eve party.

In the meantime, great mail bags full of gifts were arriving from home and there was cheer in those bundles for the men which was all out of proportion to their size. Of course there were a lot of gifts which the men could not possibly use on board a warship—probably be-speaking the peacetime nature of Santa Claus—and there was a great deal of hilarity as these gifts were shown around. However, I soon be-gan to realize that some of the men had received no gifts—the "blue" expressions on their faces were unmistakable. Again, what to do? That

"Dr Pepper is part of our national life," says this ad in the Christmas issue of **The Saturday Evening Post.** *The company could truthfully make that claim for the soft drink that was invented in 1888, a year before Coca-Cola. But like many other everyday items to which people had become accustomed—such as butter, meat, and gasoline—it was sometimes in short supply, for which this ad apologizes. The problem was mainly distribution. The big trucks that brought it to stores could never get enough gas, or rubber tires, both of which were rationed. And if a vending machine broke down, that was also a problem. National Vendors, one of the biggest suppliers of those machines, had converted all of their facilities for the duration to the manufacturing of mortar ammunition casings.*

★ ★ ★

very afternoon, a truck stopped on the dock with several large bags filled with Christmas packages. This time it was Chaplain Brooks of the District Chaplain's Office who was playing Santa Claus. It seems that Chaplain Brooks had received a great load of gifts for the men of the Navy from church people, mainly from churches in Wisconsin and Minnesota. Those gifts could not have been more fortunate or timely. We quickly drew up a list of the men who had received no gifts from home, surreptitiously addressed the packages to them, gave them to our post-office clerk, and they received a Christmas gift from some thoughtful person at home.

Christmas Eve morning, Chaplain J. W. Moore, Fleet Chaplain, drove up with nearly two hundred cans and boxes filled with delicious cookies, which had been prepared by local church people. All was ready for a grand Christmas Eve party.

Near us were two cruisers, several destroyers, LST's, mine sweepers, and an APD which had not been as fortunate in being able to have a party, so all were invited and, judging by the crowd that night, all were well represented. By party time, the hangar and well-deck were jammed and the men were draped, hanging or clinging to everything above and around. Chaplain Jerome Gill of Boston, Massachusetts, showed up with his swing band, our Christmas tree was ablaze and the party was off with a swing version of "Jingle Bells" to the accompaniment of whoops of enthusiasm from the men. Captain S. R. Shumaker, forgetting his dignity, leaped from his chair to do a shuffle-rhumba amidst gleeful whistles from everyone. Captain Shumaker endeared himself to all when he stepped to the microphone and gave all hands a cheery Christmas greeting and welcome to the NO-boat party. Being in charge of the festivities, I trotted forward at this point wearing a wreath of jingle bells around my neck, the sound of which went out through the amplifiers and gave the impression of a whole herd of reindeer hovering overhead. There were still about twenty-five gifts remaining to be

With a little imagination and much goodwill, a tropical umbrella plant, like this one on Guadalcanal, could pass muster as a Christmas tree. Instead of tinsel and colored lights there are surgical gloves and gauze.

☆ ☆ ☆

This Union Pacific ad manages to make a strong emotional point: The family is gathered to share holiday joy, but someone is missing. As with other industries affected by rationing and cutbacks, the railroads needed to maintain customer relations by linking themselves to the war effort, suggesting that "we're all in this together."

✦✦✦

distributed so I made use of a crude "spinner" numbered from 1 to 10, which I would spin for a combination of numbers. Standing by with the list of pay numbers was J. F. Jones of San Francisco, yeoman in the Pay Office, who gave me the name opposite the number which came up. This man would come forward and was required to open his gift so all could see—some uncovered oversized sweaters, etc., which was a source of great amusement to everyone.

After the gifts were distributed, there were several impromptu stunts by men of the visiting ships, and a visiting seaman gave a hilariously funny paraphrasing of the famous poem "'Twas the Night Before Christmas" beginning "'Twas the night before Christmas and all through the ship, not a creature was stirring, not even a rat . . ."—a copy of which I am still hoping to get. Then came more entertaining music from the band and the distribution of the "pogy-bait" and cookies and "gedunk" to all hands. The cookies and candy were tossed out into the crowd amid great shouting, reaching and general fun.

At this point came one of the most touching experiences I have known among the men on this ship. When the noise had subsided, I waved my hand for attention and in a few words called to mind the meaning of our rejoicing—the announcement to mankind of the birth of Jesus.

The transition was startling—where a moment before had been the raucous fun of Navy men, now there was a complete sober-faced reverence. The band struck up "It Came upon a Midnight Clear," then "Silent Night," "Joy to the World"—all the great Christmas songs. There wasn't a man there who wasn't singing, and singing from the depths of his heart—as I looked over the crowd, faces beaming with joy, sad faces and some with tears streaming unabashed. The crowd dispersed after I had given the invitation to all to attend Christmas service in the morning. Taps sounded and all hands "hit the sack" to dream perhaps a childhood-Navy dream of Santa coming down the "Stack."

Patriotism, liberty, freedom, hope, goodwill, and, most of all, light—
from a General Electric advertisement.

Christmas is a light.

> . . . a candle burning in a window.
> . . . the gleam of a star on a tree.
> . . . the light in the eyes of a child on Christmas morning.

But Christmas is more than these. Christmas is a light within.

This light shines brightest in the face of a child—but it glows *deepest* in the hearts of a father and a mother who watch the child at play.

For the light that we know in our hearts at Christmas time does not belong to Christmas alone, or to children alone.

It glows in the heart of every man in the armed forces of the United States who stands ready to give the greatest of all gifts—himself.

It shines in the heart of the worker who, through the long day, the holiday pleasures given up—gives his skill, with industry's strength, for freedom's sake.

And, in the hearts of those who gather scrap, use less sugar and coffee and tea and meat, walk to save gasoline and tires, and keep on buying *one more* U.S. War Bond.

The things we give and give up, today as Americans, are gifts of freedom and liberty and opportunity to all the world tomorrow.

☆ ☆ ☆

'Twas the Night Before Christmas
New Yorker Clement Clark Moore, who wrote "A Visit from St. Nicholas," the beloved Christmas poem, the first line of which is the title on this cartoon, could never have anticipated its use in this setting. But Christmas is for every year and everywhere, not just for nineteenth-century idyllic settings where snow glistens on rooftops.

"Hey, Sarge, I think I hear Sleighbells!"
"Nah, them's mosquitoes"

Christmas on *the* Enterpise

When these men finish cooking turkeys for Christmas dinner, they will hardly emerge from the kitchen into a typical Christmas scene. What they will see when they come up for fresh air is the vast expanse of the Pacific from the flight deck of the carrier **USS Enterprise,** the fabled "Fighting Gray Lady." The **Enterprise,** by 1943, could well have been renamed the **Avenger.** In April 1942, it accompanied and protected the ship carrying General Jimmy Doolittle and his crews to the launch point for their famous raid on Tokyo. On June 4 and 5, 1942, at the Battle of Midway, planes from the **Enterprise** damaged and sank several of the Japanese ships that participated in the raid on Pearl Harbor. And in 1945, the big ship will participate in the final bombardment of Japan itself.

★ ★ ☆

"... a whole 30 days to be with the people I loved."

NOW COMES TIME for our departure back to the States. We had to ride the train back to San Juan, and the ship we were to go home [in] was so large and loaded it couldn't come into the harbor, so we were loaded onto barges and towed to the ship. When we were all aboard the Captain told us via the public address system that we would have to sleep on deck. There just wasn't any room in the ship. He promised we would be home by Christmas. This was in 1943. We made the trip fine. No one was seasick. In fact you couldn't even feel any movement on that large ship. But things started to get bad the last day on ship. We were all in our "sun tan" uniforms we used in Puerto Rico, and now we were going very slowly up the Hudson River in December! It was overcast and very *cold*. It took most of the day to dock and get off. We were cold and hungry. We got on a troop train and went over to Camp Kilmer in Jersey. It was late in the afternoon when we arrived and got off. We thought they would take us right to the mess hall but to our dismay it was another hall. We had to have a "short arm inspection" (check for venereal disease). We wondered how they thought we could have any by traveling all this time, but we did get through and got to our barracks and finally to the mess hall. There was a surprise for us. We could eat three meals in this special mess hall, then we would go to the regular one. In this special one we could order anything we wanted and eat as much as we wanted. I mean they had everything under the sun!

We left Camp Kilmer more or less on our own. We all split up and went to our homes. I hadn't written any of my folks since I left Puerto Rico. I got off [the] train at 4th Street, walked up to Lucille's hat shop, and just walked in on her. She saw me at once and came running to me. Then she called Dad who was at work at the mill (where Mason's department store was). He came in real quick. We had a great homecoming. I had to go to Munford to see Sue. It was after dark and they had built a new highway since I had left. I had trouble finding where to turn off at Munford, but I did indeed find it. I had a whole 30 days to be with the people I loved.

Joseph A. "Buc" Craton, a cook for the U.S. Third Army, Sixty-fifth Infantry Division, spent the early part of the war in San Juan, Puerto Rico. In December 1943 he shipped out for a brief reunion with his family.

"O hear us when we cry to Thee, For those in peril on the sea!" The Naval Hymn ("Eternal Father") bespeaks the dangers of the deep, belying the calm seas in the background as a chaplain leads these enlisted men in prayer on Christmas Day. We don't know the name of this ship or where it was at the time, but German or Japanese submarines could have been lurking, wherever the location. It is a mark of how reverence had to be mixed with vigilance that one man, in the lower left of the photo, has his headphones on and is monitoring radio traffic. Who could forget that Pearl Harbor was attacked on a Sunday?

✶ ✶ ✶

Christmas Thoughts from a Seventh-Grader

The war hit Glenwood, Illinois, just as it hit other small towns across the United States. Food and materials were rationed; manufacturers turned their plants to war-related production; and schoolchildren's education about war moved from the abstract to the personal. Geography lessons focused on theaters of action, places where fathers and uncles and neighbors might be serving. Battleships and bombers became recognizable, not only to those

in the military, but also to sixth-graders. At Christmastime Glenwood students filled boxes and stockings with gifts and took them to nearby Fort Sheridan and the Great Lakes Naval Training Station for those soldiers and sailors who had not received any. And, in their own writings, youngsters revealed their personal thoughts on how the war affected their lives. Jeannette Stowe, seventh-grader, wrote on Christmas and peace.

PEACE ON CHRISTMAS DAY

Christmas day comes once a year.
But on this year's day they'll be many a tear,
For daddies, brothers and loved ones gone,
To fight a war for the come of dawn.

Each night we kneel by our beds and pray,
that the coming of dawn will not be delayed,
I know some day they'll be back to stay,
And Christmas again will be glad and gay.

There'll be no tears,
Nor empty chairs,
To fill our hearts with fear,
Nor will there be burdens to bear.

We'll all be together happy and gay,
On that glad and merry Christmas day,
With all our hopes, joys and cares,
In America our country so pure and fair.

The AMERICAN
WAR MOTHER
Official Publication of the
American War Mothers

Volume 20   DECEMBER, 1943   Number 9

Merry Christmas

★ ★ ★

The American War Mothers was a product of World War I. The organization, founded in 1917 and chartered by Congress eight years later, was originally made up of three groups: Blue Star Mothers, each of whom had at least one child in the service; Silver Star Mothers, the parents of wounded servicemen; and Gold Star Mothers, who had children who had been killed in action. Families would hang banners in a front window indicating which group applied. None was more revered than the Gold Star Mothers, whose children had made the ultimate sacrifice.

Nicknamed "ugly ducklings" by President Franklin Roosevelt, Liberty Ships were emergency cargo ships constructed for the first time during the war. "A Floating Coffin, that's what we called her," remembered one Merchant Marine. "If we took a direct hit in the engine room, nobody was going to get out alive. Hell, we didn't even hang life jackets down there. Why bother." Prefabricated, many of them built in San Francisco, Oakland, and Richmond shipyards, the Liberty Ships kept the Allied forces supplied with food, fuel, and raw materials. The volunteer civilian sailors who manned them endured some of the highest casualty rates of the war. Robert Clarke was such a sailor, a junior engineer aboard the **Theodore Fraser,** *a Liberty Ship that shuttled supplies from Algeria to Italy.*

IN DECEMBER WE RECEIVED ORDERS to proceed to Bizerte, Tunisia, to load a company of British Eighth Army Rangers, along with their equipment, for transport to Naples. We arrived in Bizerte one week

From Chaos—An Image

War often evokes unlikely images, startling contrasts. When Studs Terkel interviewed hundreds of veterans about their experiences in World War II for his book **The Good War,** *one of his witnesses was Will Stracke, a Chicago folksinger and guitarist who in 1957 founded the Old Town School of Folk Music, an institution that spawned the careers of Steve Goodman and other notable singers and writers. During his time in Italy in 1943, Stracke saw something that took his mind off the dreariness of battle.*

I remember a Christmas morning on the outskirts of Palermo. Good-conduct medals were being handed out. You'd get one if you didn't get the clap during the preceding year. We were standing in the middle of the gun positions and sang familiar Christmas carols. Someone was playing a mouth harp. Right in the middle of a carol, a boy about twelve in an Arab dress—a Mediterranean dress which probably hadn't changed in two thousand years—came through the gun position, driving his sheep. I immediately had the fantasy of seeing a boy like the young Jesus going about his work. It was a memorable experience. ★

Even Santa needs a pass to get near the docks. Ideally, security at the piers, where weapons, ammunition, and troops were loaded onto ships, ought to have been that tight, given what was at stake. But the Coast Guard, which in 1942 had been given the responsibility to provide port security, didn't have the manpower to carry it out effectively. In New York City, for example, 400 piers were deemed essential, but the 1,200 men assigned to the job, on four shifts, could cover only 300.

★ ★ ★

before Christmas, moving slowly along the rather long, narrow channel that led to the port in order to avoid the sunken ships that littered the waterway. The city of Bizerte was the epitome of destruction; the final battle for North Africa had left nothing standing. Waiting there for us were the surviving members of the Ranger company who had been on R&R after the desert campaign.

We finished loading early on Christmas Eve and were scheduled to join a small convoy for Italy on the day after Christmas. With time on our hands, we began to get acquainted. In the early evening, the merchant seamen, Navy gun crews, and British Rangers gathered together and sang Christmas carols, creating a feeling that I have never since experienced. As dusk softened the appearance of the devastated city and the arid landscape, it created an image of the Holy Land that many must have felt, for "Silent Night" and "Oh Come, All Ye Faithful" sounded different somehow.

Christmas morning was bright and warm. One of the officers conducted religious services on deck, and afterward we shared our traditional turkey dinner with the British soldiers. We spent the remainder of the day in conversation; never talking about battles past or the war ahead, but about memories of Christmases at home, so basically alike on both sides of the Atlantic.

I had struck up an acquaintance with a young British corporal, whose name and address I wrote down and subsequently lost. At one point in our conversation I mentioned that I had once collected stamps and coins. He exclaimed that it reminded him of something he had found and wanted to show me, so he went to fetch it from his pack. On his return, he opened his hand to show me a small, thick, brass-colored coin. I picked it up and examined it. On one side was the profile of a Roman emperor, with an inscription in Latin around the edge; the design on the other side was not readily identifiable. The coin was canted to one side, as if the mold had slipped in minting. The corporal said that he had found the coin in one of the Roman ruins during the campaign, perhaps exposed by shelling or some other disturbance connected with the troop movements. He said I could keep the coin, that he would probably lose it anyway. "Consider it a Christmas present," he said and would not listen when I refused to accept it. Later, I gave him a carton of cigarettes that I had been saving, but it seemed a rather feeble exchange on my part.

We reached Naples on New Year's Day and immediately discharged our cargo of troops and equipment. There was a good deal of waving and shouted good-byes as the troops moved onto the bombed-out dock and disappeared around the corner of the rubble-strewn street.

By this time the Germans had decided to make a stand at the Garigliano River, some 35 miles north of Naples. They lost this position to the Allies in a horrendous battle on January 17 and 18. Our ship's captain later received word that the British Ranger company we had brought in—whose job was to "open up" the enemy for the other troops to advance—had been killed almost to the man in this battle.

It is ironic that the coin that was originally taken from Rome to Africa as part of a campaign of war was discovered as part of another act of war; and that its foreign discoverer should lose his life so close to the coin's point of origin.

Occasionally I look at the coin, but I try not to dwell on the tragic circumstances that took the life of the young man who gave it to me. Instead I think of that Christmas day in 1943, with the camaraderie, companionship, and comfort that existed for the short time that we could forget the war.

By Christmas 1943, the personnel of the Eighth Air Force had grown to 200,000 strong, with the ability to marshal 2,000 four-engine bombers in its daylight strategic bombing campaign against Germany. But in this photo, one member of this vast air armada is alone with his God this Christmas season in the chancery of a small church near his base in England. The advance party of history's greatest air unit arrived in Britain in February 1942, flew its first combat mission over occupied Europe that July 4, and sent its first heavy bombers into action, over Rouen, France, in August. The lead pilot on that mission, Paul Tibbets, would play a major role aboard the **Enola Gay** *in the atom bombing of Hiroshima in 1945.*

★ ★ ★

A Busload of Strangers

Christmas during wartime—it brought people closer together, perhaps a little more tolerant of annoyances that would otherwise seem formidable. Olive Nowak remembers a bus ride from a small, southern Minnesota town on Christmas Eve 1943.

It didn't promise to be the best of Christmas Eves—America was in the midst of World War II.

By the time I arrived at the little bus depot in Albert Lea, Minnesota, a crowd of impatient travelers, many of them servicemen, were waiting for the bus. I was eager to get home to my family. My younger brother was already talking about enlisting in the Marines. This might be the last Christmas we would be together for a long time. My thoughts were also on a certain soldier overseas who was very special to me.

There was a collective sigh of relief as the bus rounded the corner, then dismay when after a few passengers departed, we saw it was still full. The bus driver shook his head sadly as he told us there wasn't any more room.

Suddenly a young sailor called out, "Hey, if there's a cute blonde out there, I'll be glad to hold her on my lap!" Amid the laughter of the crowd, other bus passengers then began calling to the driver, "Put them all on—we'll share our seats so no one has to be left behind." Within minutes, there were three and four people snuggled into seats for two, some people sitting in others' laps.

As our busload of strangers sped through the night, someone began softly singing Silent Night. One by one we all joined in, until every passenger was singing—Joy to the World, Away in a Manger; White Christmas, I'll Be Home for Christmas. We laughed, we sang, we shared candy and cookies. And we watched, misty-eyed, as departing servicemen, who only a few minutes before had been so cool, cried unashamedly as they were embraced by waiting wives, mothers, and fathers. When the bus reached my destination, the remaining passengers shouted out, "Merry Christmas, Happy New Year!"

When the war ended, my "special" soldier returned home, and we were married. Since then, we have spent many happy Christmas Eves together with our children, and, more recently, our grandchildren. Yet I doubt if I'll ever again experience the same feeling of peace and contentment that came over me that night during the war. As I stood there, watching the bus disappear into the night, I was eager to be home but reluctant to break the spell of fellowship. The snow had stopped falling, and the sky was studded with stars. I thought of the awe that must have gripped the hearts of those long-ago shepherds who had once gazed at a star over Bethlehem. And I understood that even in the midst of war there could still be "Peace on earth, good will to men." ★

I WELL REMEMBER the period before Christmas 1943. Two things in particular stand out. First, the weather. Anyone who was asked to lead one of those midwinter forays knew the odds were greatly against his being able to complete his mission with any degree of success. We had not got our pathfinder equipment set up then—that came a few months later—and so at that time we could not bomb by instruments. Each trip out was apt to be characterized by a number of midair collisions between bombers climbing through heavy overcast. There were cases of ships loading up in freezing cloud layers and spinning in under the tremendous weight of gas, bombs, and ice. There were always men who returned with frostbitten hands, faces, and feet. Normally these were the ones who were lucky enough to get over the target. We were short of the proper number of electric flying suits with electric gloves and boots. Every time some men would have to go without and would have to be hospitalized because of frostbite.

The other thing I particularly remember was about Christmas itself. At the Government's urging, most of the folks back home had mailed our Christmas packages early. Many of the packages arrived in late November. I was taught to make quite a holiday out of opening Christmas packages, and I had come to feel it kind of a sin to open them before Christmas. Kind friends and members of my family saw to it that I had many packages to open. My problem each time I was up for a mission was to decide whether or not to open my presents. I always felt there was a pretty fair chance I wouldn't come back, and it seemed stupid to leave the packages laying around unopened. I had seen the unopened Christmas packages of many of my missing friends marked "Return to Sender." I went through that indecision many times. Each time I would go to bed leaving the packages unopened. In the icy cold of the black morning when I was called out to fly I would wonder again whether I would be back to see them once more. Strange that a man my age should spend as much time as I did debating the matter of Christmas packages!

The truth, I guess, was that those packages were the most recent tie between me and loved ones back home. It was not what was in them, but that they represented so much time and effort and affection that caused me to make almost a fetish of them. Whatever they contained they were expressions straight from the hearts of those dearest to me;

From the beginning of U.S. involvement in the European war, bomber pilot Philip Ardery had challenged the odds; he had flown inches above the chimneys of oil refineries in Romania, dodged anti-aircraft guns over Germany, Italy, and Austria, and had, on many occasions, confronted "a bedlam of bombers flying in all directions, some actually on fire, many with smoking engines, some with great gaping holes in them or huge chunks of wing or rudder gone." Christmas 1943 offered a feeling of respite from the fear and growing anxiety that the next mission might be his last.

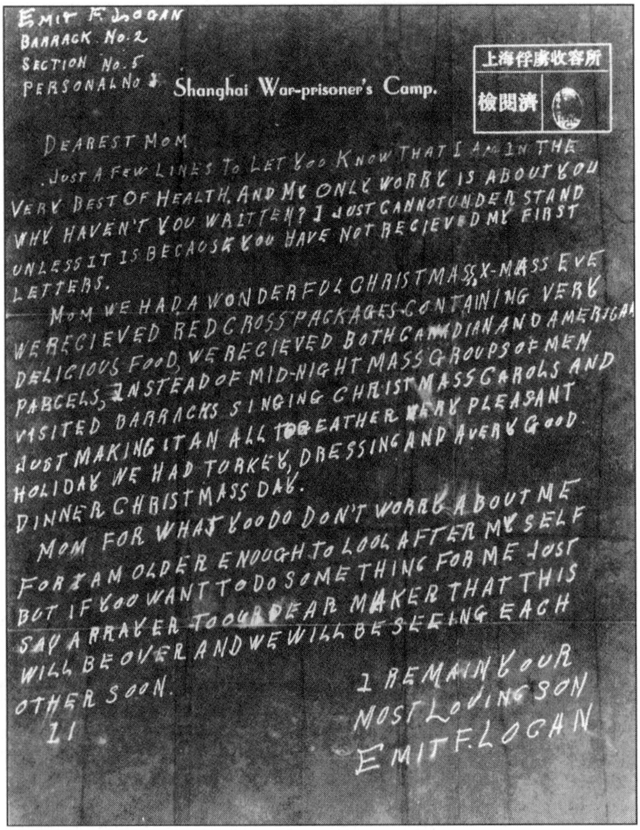

The handwritten letter reads:

EMIT F. LOGAN
BARRACK No. 2
SECTION No. 5
PERSONAL No. — Shanghai War-prisoner's Camp.

上海俘虜収容所
檢閲済

DEAREST MOM

Just a few lines to let you know that I am in the very best of health, and my only worry is about you. Why haven't you written? I just cannot understand unless it is because you have not recieved my first letters.

Mom we had a wonderful Christmass. X-Mass Eve we recieved Red Cross packages containing very delicious food, we recieved both Canadian and American parcels, Instead of mid-night mass groups of men visited barracks singing Christmass Carols and Just making it an all together very pleasant Holiday we had Torkey, dressing and a very good Dinner Christmass day.

Mom for what you do don't worry about me for I am older enough to look after my self but if you want to do something for me Just say a prayer to our Dear Maker that this will be over and we will be seeing each other soon.

I REMAIN YOUR
MOST LOVING SON
EMIT F. LOGAN

The thought of spending Christmas in a prisoner-of-war camp is a bleak one. In Emit F. Logan's case, the Red Cross has offered some comfort with food packages, but Emit is worried about not hearing from his mother. He paints a fairly decent picture of how he has been treated, but it's hard to say if he's just appeasing the censor.

☆ ☆ ☆

and to open them before Christmas was to destroy their magic. I was true to my principle, and the Lord rewarded me by bringing me home on all those occasions. The end of that dilemma was that on Christmas morning I found myself alone in my room sitting on the floor opening presents. I don't remember what I got, but I felt closer to those at home at that moment than I had since I left the States.

Our station had been selected for a Christmas broadcast over CBS which afforded excitement. I was particularly interested in the broadcast because Edward R. Murrow and Larry LeSueur came up to run it. I had met Larry some time before. He had come up a month early for a short visit to make advance arrangements. I had cornered him and got him on the subject of politics, the war, and Russia. Larry had spent a long time in Russia and was the best authority I ever had a chance to talk to. LeSueur and Murrow were too busy on that occasion for me to see much of them, but after I renewed my old acquaintance with Larry he invited me to stay with him next time I came to London. I was pleased at the prospect of having a chance to talk about things I hadn't discussed in a long time.

The Christmas broadcast was a huge success. Many officers and enlisted men had an opportunity to say a few words to reassure their families back home that they were well and as happy as Americans can ever be so far from home. I was convinced of the dedication of the American newsmen. They performed an immensely important role, and the ones I saw had a conscientiousness about their work which was quite impressive.

". . . there'll be the family, but no you . . ."

After graduating from the University of Chicago in 1939, Alfred de Grazia began a career as a teacher of law and politics. After entering the war and surviving six campaigns from Germany to Africa, he finished his military years as commander of psychological warfare of the Seventh Army. He later became an esteemed author of works in political science, history, and education, and a professor at such universities as Brown, Stanford, and New York University. At Christmas 1943, Jill Oppenheim, de Grazia's wife, a Smith College graduate, University of Chicago student, and a gifted writer who bore him seven children, penned one of hundreds of letters that raised his spirits. Through the war years, the two exchanged some 1,200 pieces of correspondence, constituting 775,000 words.

Darling—Tuesday

I've already written you a fairly long Air Mail letter earlier this evening. But not trusting any form of mail these days, and wanting to talk to you anyway, I'll put off bedtime a little longer. I had some sewing to do tonight & tried to lighten the hateful task by listening to the radio, which dripped Xmas cheer all over the rug. As a result, I am cheerless in the exact proportions to which Bob Hope et al were full of holiday mirth. There is a peculiar psychology in missing someone you love—the pain becomes greatest during the times you deviate from the ordinary, & to most people, distasteful, routine of living—the Sundays, the feast days, the idle moments just before you go to bed. Last Christmas seemed incomplete because we had to spend it in an unfamiliar clime, away from any of our families.

☆ ☆ ☆
By 1943, the image of Santa had been drafted into use as a symbol of reassurance that the men and women of the armed forces were being well cared for at this special time of year.

★ 1943 ★

How ungrateful I was! This Christmas there'll be the family, but no you—an infinitely less desirable state of affairs, even though I'll have the enviable role of playing Momma & hostess to the folks, because they'll be coming down here for dinner. But I almost wish the baby would start coming Christmas Eve, so I could be preoccupied and therefore spared these poignant thoughts of you on Christmas Day. However, I'm not forgetting that the pain I feel for your absence is yours many times over, since your Christmas has all the disadvantages—a strange country, no family, no Jill, and a natural apprehension about the baby. I almost wish you could have the baby (painlessly) so you wouldn't have to worry about me. It would be pleasant, anyway, to see the consternation of 5th Army medics if that were to happen.

Stay healthy, dear one.

All my love,

Jill

*While cards between loved ones back home and their boy or husband on the front are what we most associate with Christmas in wartime, service personnel also exchanged greetings among one another. This V-Mail Christmas greeting was sent from the most appropriate place one could imagine: the actual location of the birth being celebrated. (But despite the lovely, tranquil scene, note the place for the censor's stamp at the upper left, a reminder that **any** kind of message could be a potentially subversive one during war.) The actual scene is now a tranquil one only because the British had stopped German general Erwin Rommel's tank force at El Alamein in mid-1942 and, joining with the American forces that landed under the command of General Eisenhower, defeated the Germans in Africa by May of this year.*

★ ★ ★

In 1903, Henry—Hap—Arnold entered West Point; in that same year the Wright Brothers flew at Kitty Hawk. After graduation and a tour in the infantry in the Philippines, Arnold volunteered for flight training with the Wrights in Dayton, Ohio. The stint in Dayton launched a meteoric career. He pioneered innovative uses of the airplane in reconnaissance, established an early high-altitude record, trained pilots, and promoted the aviation industry. In World War II, Hap Arnold had become Commanding General of the Army Air Forces and was an eminent leader in shaping a supreme American airpower. In December 1943, with the war still uncertain but with American pilots demonstrating great skill and courage, he sent them a Christmas message.

To All Personnel of the Army Air Forces:

At Christmas last year we began to see light after the long darkness of the first year of the war. Confident of your enormous efforts as individuals and as a fighting force, I knew that we could expect with assurance a new year that would be a bright year and a proud year. We in the AAF have found it so. The hopes we held were abundantly realized. The confidence we felt proved to be well-founded.

This Christmas we have all that to be thankful for. Our hopes for the future are very high. In the consciousness of hard jobs well done, I hope every man and woman in the AAF will have at heart a Merry Christmas even in surroundings that may be strange.

Christmas Eve and Christmas Day some of you may find yourselves engaged in deadly combat. Many of you will be suffering hardships and dangers in situations as unlike Christmas as any you ever imagined. Very few of you will be able to spend Christmas as we would all wish to spend it. That will come again on those Christmases after we have finished the job.

With these thoughts in mind I send my Christmas and New Year's greetings to every one of you,

General Henry "Hap" Arnold

★ ★ ★

wherever you are. As you know, the coming year will bring the most decisive days of our time, the most decisive of centuries to come perhaps. I am fully confident that you are equal to the challenge. Your courage and endurance, your devotion and your labor have carried us strong and safe and brought us one year nearer victory and realization of things for which Christmas stands.

A Veteran's Poem to His Son

Military service and combat experience in individual families often spanned generations. Spanish-American War veterans fathered children who served in World War I who fathered children who served in World War II. In 1943 Charles Dibb, a police official, wrote a poem about saying good-bye to a son who had enlisted in the navy. **The American War Mother** *published the poem in its Christmas 1943 issue.*

> You stood there, Son, in your navy blues,
> with your cap kinda over one eye,
> And I know that I didn't say very much,
> maybe just, "Chin up, and goodbye;"
> I pondered, should I have talked to you,
> about cautioning on wrong and observing the right?
> But then, it didn't seem real that my boy
> was a man and going away to the fight.
>
> And, Son, my thoughts drifted back twenty-five
> years, and the day I thought me a man;
> And that railway platform where I stood,
> just a kid in the army's tan.
> Your grandfather there shook my hand,
> and said, "Goodbye, my son."
> So I wonder if he thought, as I left for
> France, of advice that would not come.

But I'm wondering now, if he didn't just
	know, as I rolled away on those wheels,
That I'd never morally wander far, but
	sorta hang on close to his ideals,
For the things unsaid, were the things
	he had been teaching me for 18 years;
That I never would lean very far from
	them, nor cause him many fears.

So, now my hope is that Mother and I
	have been as capable in that way,
For because of Dad and Mother, I came
	through all right, so I'm sure I'll see the day
When you'll be home once more, and in
	shaking your hand I'll know,
That because of my Dad, just "Goodbye,
	Son," was enough when I saw you go.

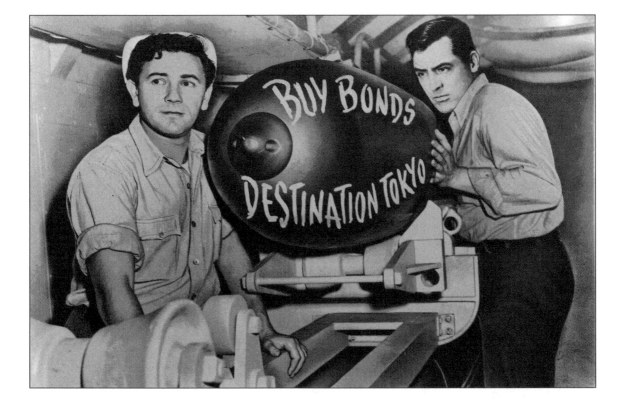

Christmas Dance at the Negro Service Club

The date is December 23, 1943, and the place is a Negro Service Club, where "White Christmas" must surely have had a mixed meaning. It is still five years before President Truman will issue an executive order desegregating the armed forces, and like most everything else in America, people in the army and all its supporting institutions, including places of rest and relaxation, are separated by race. In the Navy, African-Americans can serve only in the mess units (a member of one such unit was given the first Silver Medal awarded in World War II, for heroism at Pearl Harbor). A separate flying school for blacks at Tuskegee Institute graduates pilots—the famous Tuskegee Airmen—who will see action. Late in the war, the 761st Tank Battalion will become the first black unit to fight in Europe, liberating several concentration camps with General Patton's Third Army.

☆ ☆ ☆

No More Christmas for Tom

Stanley Frankel was an unlikely soldier. Drafted into the U.S. army ten months before the attack on Pearl Harbor, he had led student rallies at Northwestern University calling for nonparticipation in the European war. But after three and a half years and five major battles as an infantryman, he had achieved the rank of major and had survived, unlike several of his friends—men such as Rodger Young, who gave up his life to save twenty men on his patrol, and Bob Harley, hit by a mortar shell in New Georgia while eating C rations with Frankel.

Years after his war service, Frankel used his journal, some letters, and many painful memories to record his war experiences in a book, which he dedicated to his grandson Adam "in the hope and prayer that what happened to me and my generation will never, never, never happen to Adam and his."

A MONTH AGO, our boys departed from New Georgia. The fighting was all over. We had helped take the airport. Before New Georgia it was the Russell Islands. Before that, Guadalcanal. We've spent one Christmas on the Fiji Islands, so a tropical Yuletide will be no novelty.

We are now behind the front lines, somewhere. We are re-organizing, getting set, shadow boxing with machine guns, doing roadwork in jungle terrain, sharpening our punches on a 200-yard rifle range. We can't promise that we'll be at it again December 25. We don't know. I'm writing this as if a foxhole Christmas is the prospect.

That's why there'll be little outward sign of holiday. We are ground-bound infantry. We will be too close to Japanese lines to make even crude church services feasible. There will be Christmas, however, in hearts and minds. When you lie in a hole built up by bamboo logs and coral and the shrapnel whines overhead, you become converted by that rude shelter, far more than you have ever been by lofty cathedrals. The man ahead of you in an elongated squad column is knocked down by machine-gun fire. You want to believe that there is someone up there who is looking out for you in future ambushes.

The cross-like four-man holes are dug, the outposts are drawn in, the fields of fire are cut, and the cans of vegetable hash are opened. Tastes pretty good, even if this same C ration has been your breakfast, lunch and supper the past month. The boys will talk about Christmas

School 160
Alborn, Minnesota
December 29, 1943

Admiral Halsey
S. Pacific Headquarters
Fleet Post Office
San Francisco, California

Dear Sir:
The Duluth Tribune tells us that the 14th battalion of Seabees has come home for Christmas after working on Guadalcanal. My husband is in the 63 Battalion which also was on G during the "blitz." He's been overseas almost 18 months with only a brief 10 weeks in this country (without leave coming). There's a lot of talk about "morale." I'm sure Kaing A. Heine cm/1c 63 Const. Bn. Co. C. could use the boost in morale

a visit to the States would naturally give, but what about his country school teacher wife who tries to do her part in these isolated north Minnesota woods (instead Ja war plant where you'd see people at least). It is I who really needs a boost in morale. When will it be possible to help us both?
Yours truly,
Fannie M. Heine
(Mrs. L. A. Heine)

It may be that "all is fair in love and war," but that doesn't mean that war is fair. Strategy, tactics, logistics, and the need for specific men and materials at specific places and times governs all, even when it's the Christmas season. That's small consolation to a wife at holiday time who has not seen her husband in far too many months. Mrs. Heine, a Minnesota schoolteacher, apparently believes in the old adage of going "straight to the top." And so she makes her case directly to Admiral Halsey. Halsey, whom General Douglas MacArthur called "the greatest fighting admiral" of the war, was given command of U.S. naval forces in the South Pacific in 1942. Did he grant this lonely wife's Christmas wish? We don't know.

☆ ☆ ☆

turkeys, and the sadists will recall sumptuous Christmas meals . . . a hundred years ago, it seems . . . lingering gently on each bit of drumstick and each cranberry.

A few boys will break the rules. They'll whisper about old times, about other Christmas Eves. The captain will tell them harshly to "keep your mouths shut," but the CO [commanding officer] doesn't know who's talking and he isn't allowed out of his hole to find out.

What do the boys think underneath this small talk? You guess it. I believe in each soldier out here there's that insatiable yearning to be

The soldier depicted in the process of becoming the Coca-Cola Santa Claus will be carrying on in an important tradition. The image of Santa that evolved through the 1930s in Coca-Cola ads—a stout fellow with glowing rosy cheeks and an ear-to-ear smile in his flame-red suit—became the one that Americans adopted as the true picture of St. Nick, and remains so to this day.

☆ ☆ ☆

home, safe and sound, warm and dry. They don't whimper, but they'll complain about being away so long.

Will it be a white Christmas by 1944? Or 1945? Or 1946? Do they pray more fervently on Christmas Eve? I guess they do. It's a holy night and that might give a little extra consideration tonight. As the enemy planes with their weird off-beat motors fly overhead and the searchlight beams finger them in the sky and the ack-ack tracers (like Christmas lights) shoot up and the bomb bays open and spit downward, then a fellow gets a little desperate and prays tonight or any night.

Sleep. Day soon breaks. The platoon sergeant reads the gist of the notes he took at the CO's meeting. Objective is three miles away on the knoll of that hill. The men look on bitterly. One frowns: "Merry Christmas!"

We start our approach march with one squad preceding the main advance guard. The enemy dual-purpose gun shells us a little, more a nuisance than with any lethal value. We plod on slowly, each file looking toward its side of the jungle for machine guns and snipers. Suddenly a shot like a cap pistol cracks out. We hit the ground, wiggle toward the brush along the road, and look and wait. We can't do anything else. We think of home and Christmas again. The point-squad has spotted the sniper. Lots of firing. They made sure he's dead even if he won't fall out of the tree. But there's a call for litter bearers and Corporal Thompson is lugged off with a shoulder wound. He's glad he's out of it for a time.

We find a pillbox, surround it, throw in everything. Finally roll a couple of hand grenades into the slits. We collect our wounded. One boy is dead. We hang around and help dig the grave while the chaplain scurries forward and finishes it off. It's Tom, the blond kid, whose letters I've censored for the past six months.

No one cries, because this is old stuff. Carl, the dead boy's foxhole partner, looks up at the lieutenant and kind of apologizes for sentiment: "No more Christmases for Tom, eh sir?"

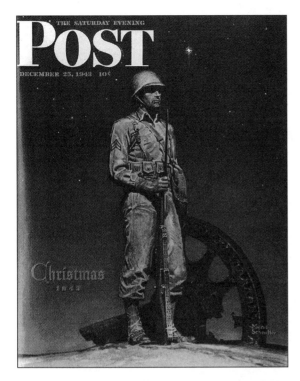

Three of the most popular general-interest magazines of the time, **The Saturday Evening Post, Collier's,** *and* **Liberty,** *all captured an aspect of Christmas 1943 on their covers. A lone sentry stands watch, almost etched under a starlit sky in the dramatic* **Saturday Evening Post** *Christmas cover. The* **Collier's** *cover depicts a GI Santa Claus bringing Christmas joy to a little foreign boy. Lest we forget, the joy of Christmas is tempered by the banner of the Gold Star Mothers, reflected in the Christmas tree decoration, announcing that this home has lost a boy in the service, as shown on the cover of* **Liberty.** *The magazines combined fiction, nonfiction, and humor. Their publishing mix aimed to offer something for everyone.*

☆ ☆ ☆

These soldiers, celebrating Christmas on Bougainville, one of the Solomon Islands, would fit in well in the war films that Hollywood was turning out at the time. They are all from Ohio, except the man standing at the left; he's from Brooklyn. Members of "C" Battery of the Thirty-seventh Division, these GIs are playing a role in the grand strategy that will bring the Allies up through the Solomons, beginning with Guadalcanal in 1942, to the Philippines next year, and ultimately to Japan itself. The Thirty-seventh landed on Bougainville only one month earlier, and their job in the next few months will be to hold a large enough slice of the big island so that an Allied air base can be constructed, a springboard to further conquests up the line of islands leading to Emperor Hirohito's front door.

☆ ☆ ☆

A Different Perspective

 Millions of individuals in the United States in late 1943 wrote letters home; some of the men were German prisoners of war. During the early months of the war, the U.S. Army began constructing internment facilities for captured Axis troops; most of the camps were extensions of military bases. In central Louisiana, Camp Ruston, built expressly as an internment facility, began accepting prisoners in late 1942, many from Erwin Rommel's Afrika Korps, as well as Luftwaffe pilots and U-boat crew members. The camp eventually housed over four thousand men. POW Hans W. Kaiser sends Christmas greetings home.

To my loved ones at home!

. . . We celebrated Christmas again, and again I am not with you. But that's only the outside appearance. All my thoughts (. . .) belong to you and therefore you are with me as well. I still did not get mail from you so all there is is the worries about you. I am doing very good. We started Christmas Eve with a church service. Then we had the celebration. The Führer (. . .) gave all of us a money gift. We received 88 German cigarettes, tobacco, and cookies from the Red Cross. We really appreciate it. We know that home won't forget the sons and we won't forget home. Our thoughts are with you, the Führer and all our comrades at the front lines.

Yesterday morning we had church service again. We spend time playing cards and telling stories. Today in the afternoon there is a soccer game and tonight there will be a concert. I wonder if this Christmas was the last one in war? To my loved ones, I send a thousand greetings.

Yours
Hans

Insufferably Hot: Christmas in New Guinea

In the land of the setting sun, Christmas 1943 seemed to many visitors like Hell itself—sweltering heat; torrential rain that turned streams into dangerous walls of water ripping away everything in their paths; thousands of exhausted troops taking on the swamps, the disease, and each other. In October, after subjecting Japanese troops in New Guinea to relentless bombardment, General MacArthur's forces landed on New Britain and began a powerful, systematic assault that would bring them to within striking distance of the Philippines. **New York Times** *reporter Frank Kluckhohn filed a Christmas report from a different world.*

OUT HERE THIS YEAR Christmas is just another day. It is not only as hot as that one insufferable day each summer at home, but damp also. Everyone is wringing wet.

Overhead pilots are winging their way in Liberators, Mitchells, Marauders, Lightnings and Thunderbolts toward Japanese targets as they did yesterday and the day before, and the day before that, and the chances are good that at least one crew or individual will not come back.

On New Britain, in the dank, treacherous jungle, the Sixth Army Yanks, tired of eleven days of fighting since the landing, are at it again and enemy guns are going.

American servicemen stationed in Britain prepare for an Orphans' Christmas party they are giving for fifty English children. The soldiers are donating part of their weekly candy rations and contributing bright Christmas wrappings to the festivities. On the whole, American GIs earned a reputation for friendliness and personal generosity not only among friendly populations but also when they occupied former enemies Germany and Italy after the war.

★ ★ ★

On New Britain also some of the lads are sleeping in foxholes, drinking stagnant, warm water from their canteens and eating hash cold from tins.

Tireless Navy boys, operating landing craft, are doing their shift, carrying supplies to the fighting Americans and Australians. For we are fighting a vicious, non-Christian enemy and there is no relaxation for a Christian holiday.

But these lads know that they are making possible something approaching a merry Christmas at home and they are getting satisfaction out of that.

As soldiers, not actually in the line, open the packages from home which they have been guarding, in some cases for weeks, they are thinking of their families and friends and wishing it were possible to be with them, and in many cases they are missing the snow to which in this holiday season they are accustomed.

Most of the men now here are leaving special celebrations to the supply troops and to those still in training on the Australian mainland.

The natives, in laplaps—multi-colored cloths wound sarong-like from the waist to midleg—and with hyacinths in their hair, have erected bamboo churches with small altars in many parts of New Guinea and chaplains of all denominations are giving services for those able to attend. There is some hymn singing at these jungle shrines.

Many outfits will have turkey dinners but not all, for ships in the past few weeks have been loaded with supplies for the fighting men. All of them had turkey on Thanksgiving Day.

Even though this is largely a routine day out here and there is little Christmas atmosphere, the lads hope, as they go grimly about the business of making war, that the New Year will see the crushing of Adolf Hitler's Germany and that the end of the year will see Japan at least well on the way to defeat.

For insurance companies, a "personal relationship" with current policyholders and the prospect of acquiring new customers is important for business. Warm Christmas wishes conveyed through ads, in 1943 just as today, were one good way of achieving this goal.

✦ ✦ ✦

Internment

Photographer Ansel
Adams, famed for his
high-contrast images
of the American
West, took the photo
of this Japanese-
American family of
six celebrating Christ-
mas at the Manzanar
War Relocation
Center in Owens
Valley, California.
There were ten reloca-
tion centers, in Califor-
nia, Arizona, Utah,
Idaho, Colorado,
Wyoming, and
Arkansas. The resi-
dents of the relocation
centers were forced to
leave their homes on
the West Coast, sell
their businesses at
ruinous prices, and
travel hundreds of
miles into the interior
to spend the duration
of the war in poor,
makeshift accommo-
dations. Families
had to cope as best
they could.
★★★

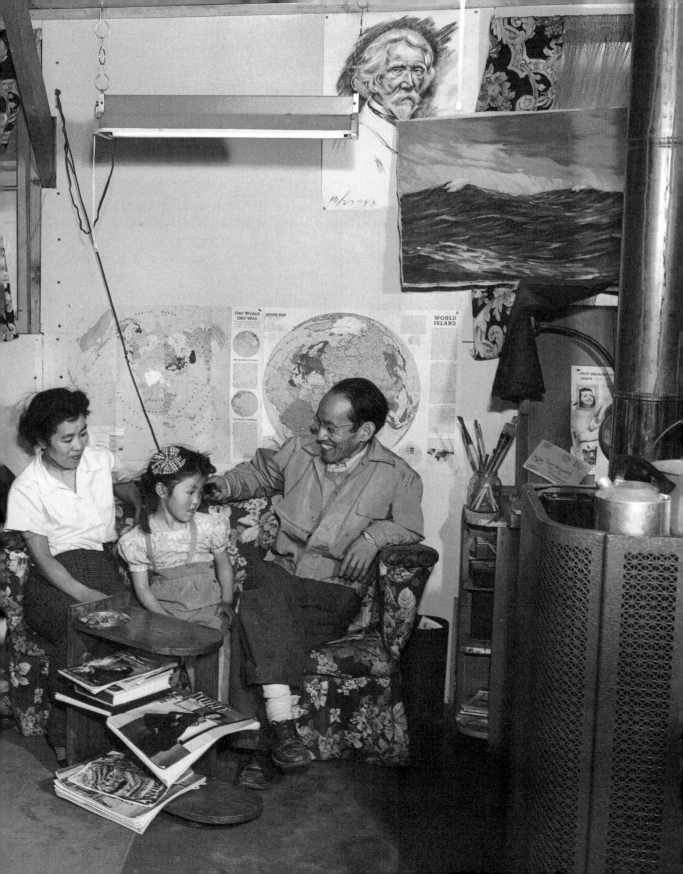

A Young Voice from an Internment Camp

For Japanese-Americans the war brought a different kind of pain. Detained by the Justice Department, they were separated from their families and detained in internment camps run by the War Relocation Authority. Tetsuzo Hirasaki was one of those uprooted from his home in California and sent to live out the war in a relocation center in Poston, Arizona. In late December 1943, Tetsuzo wrote a letter to a special friend, Clara Breed, the Children's Librarian at the San Diego Public Library. Outraged by the treatment of the Japanese-American community, Clara Breed spoke out against the injustice and remained in contact with those children who had used the library, exchanging letters, sending gifts, and offering encouragement and hope.

At the Granada Relocation Center in Amache, Colorado, the two Miyake children, Peggy and Bobby, have no Christmas tree because none has been made available for them. Nevertheless, their mother has brought them the warmth of Christmas with presents, and one of them is very special: a picture of their father, Bill, who is in the army. Despite their treatment, about 25,000 Japanese-Americans served in the armed forces in World War II, and the all-Japanese-American 442nd Combat Team would become the most decorated unit, relative to its size, in American history.

☆ ☆ ☆

Poston, Arizona
December 29, 1943

Dear Miss Breed,

A rather belated Season's Greetings.

Thank you ever so much for the gifts. It certainly is a treat to receive such rare items—especially the Hershey Bar!

Dad sends his thanks, too. He sends his best wishes to you and your mother for the coming year. He is getting along fine.

Because of the rough handling of the Christmas rush mail here in Poston, I have delayed in sending you and your mother a couple of Poston Products until a substantial container had been made. We have been so busy cutting hair that's all we have time for during the day. Everyone wants to look his best for the New Year.

I am again attending shorthand class at night and with homework to do, I am quite busy. Especially when I am trying to catch up with the sleep lost at Tule Lake. Add the correspondence that I have neglected and I am so busy that I have not been able to practice my music. That has been neglected for nearly two months now so I have just about completely forgotten all that I had learned.

It rained Christmas night and I couldn't help but to think back to that Christmas two short and yet long years ago when we were all together—now there are hundred of miles separating us. By the way the morning mail (Monday) brought a card from Eleanor! I must be getting clairvoyant.

Sincerely Yours,
Ted

P.S. Do you have any of the soy sauce left? T.H.

1944

✶ ✶ ✶

I N THE SPRING of 1944 Group Captain James Stagg, chief meteorologist for the Royal Air Force, made what some believe was the most important weather prediction in history—gradual clearing on June 6 in Normandy. On D day 150,000 Allied Expeditionary forces stormed the beaches—their objective: to open a second major European front in the battle against the Nazis. General Dwight D. Eisenhower, commander of the United Forces, said, "This landing is but the opening phase of the campaign in Western Europe. Great battles lie ahead. I call upon all who love freedom to stand with us now." They did.

Among those who participated were thousands of black Americans who played a critical role in Allied successes, both on the home front and on the front lines. In July Army Lieutenant Jack Roosevelt Robinson (aka Jackie Robinson), an African-American of great personal courage as well as athletic prowess, boarded a military bus at Fort Hood and was told to sit in the back. He refused. Later, he faced a court-martial. He was acquitted.

In August the Allies took back Paris. A U.S. soldier wrote later: "As long as I live I don't guess I'll ever see a parade like that . . . we were marching twenty-four abreast down the Champs Elysees and we had a helluva time trying to march, because the whole street was jammed with people laughing and yelling and crying and singing."

In September Frank Capra's movie *Arsenic and Old Lace* premiered; it starred Cary Grant, Raymond Massey, and Peter Lorre. The following month, Ozzie and Harriet Nelson made their debut on CBS Radio with "The Adventures of Ozzie and Harriet." The Martha Graham ballet *Appalachian Spring*, with music by Aaron Copland, also premiered in the fall, with Graham in a leading role. And "The Roy Rogers Show" was first heard on the Mutual Broadcasting System. Singing along with Roy, "The King of the Cowboys," were the Sons of the Pioneers.

On November 7 the nation elected President Roosevelt to an unprecedented fourth term in office; Roosevelt defeated Thomas E. Dewey.

In mid-December the Germans attempted to drive a wedge between British and American troops with a massive winter offensive in the Ardennes Forest of Belgium. A small town called Bastogne, the body in an octopus network of roads, became a vital target. Stubbornly but tenuously, American forces held. The siege would later be known as "the Battle of the Bulge," where hundreds of thousands of men and women spent Christmas.

From "somewhere in Germany," the Second Infantry sends Christmas greetings. This fighting unit first saw action in World War I at Belleau-Wood, and helped to occupy Germany after that war. In peacetime it was stationed at Fort Sam Houston, Texas, but in 1943 was moved to Ireland as Operation Overlord took shape. The Second Infantry Division went ashore at Omaha Beach in Normandy the day after D day.

☆ ☆ ☆

By December 22, 1944, German forces had surrounded the Belgian town of Bastogne. Unable to receive supplies by air because of terrible weather conditions, American troops still held on. A German "surrender party," displaying a white flag, approached the perimeter and was taken to a command post. The party delivered an ultimatum—give up or face a "total annihilation." When the message reached Division Commander General Anthony McAuliffe, he had a response that has gone down in World War II lore.

Headquarters 101st Airborne Division
Office of the Division Commander
24 December 1944

What's Merry about all this, you ask? We're fighting—it's cold— we aren't home. All true but what has the proud Eagle Division accomplished with its worthy comrades of the 10th Armored Division, the 705th Tank Destroyer Battalion and all the rest? just this: We have stopped cold everything that has been thrown at us from the North, East, South and West. We have identifications from four German Panzer Divisions, two German Infantry Divisions and one German Parachute Division. These units, spearheading the last desperate German lunge, were headed straight west for key points when the Eagle Division was hurriedly ordered to stem the advance. How effectively this was done will be written in history; not alone in our Division's glorious history but in World history. The Germans actually did surround us, their radios blared our doom. Their Commander demanded our surrender in the following impudent arrogance.

December 22nd 1944

To the U.S.A. Commander of the encircled town of Bastogne.

The fortune of war is changing. This time the U.S.A. forces in and near Bastogne have been encircled by strong German armored units. More German armored units have crossed the river Ourthe near Ortheuville, have taken Marche and reached St. Hubert by passing through Hombres-Sibret-Tillet. Libramont is in German hands.

There is only one possibility to save the encircled U.S.A. troops from total annihilation: that is the honorable surrender of the encircled town. In order to think it over a term of two hours will be granted beginning with the presentation of this note.

If this proposal should be rejected one German Artillery Corps and six heavy A. A. Battalions are ready to annihilate the U.S.A.

A scene from the film **Since You Went Away,** *producer David O. Selznick's saga of the home front. The movie begins with Claudette Colbert seeing her husband off to war. Over the film's three hours friends and neighbors cope with separation, loss, and the difficulty of leading a normal life under wartime conditions. At the end, Colbert's husband has been reported missing in action. It's Christmas Eve. The family has gathered to take what cheer they can. Then the phone rings. It's him, he's safe, and he's coming home. In the fadeout, Colbert walks out into a snowy street scene as the audience hears her thoughts in voice-over: "I've let go of the past, Tim. . . . I'm not afraid to face the future now, becuase you'll be here to share it with me . . . the new world . . . which we'll make better than the old."*

☆ ☆ ☆

troops in and near Bastogne. The order for firing will be given immediately after this two hours term.

All the serious civilian losses caused by this Artillery fire would not correspond with the well known American humanity.

The German Commander

The German Commander received the following reply:

22 December 1944
To the German Commander:
    NUTS!

The American Commander

Allied Troops are counterattacking in force. We continue to hold Bastogne. By holding Bastogne we assure the success of the Allied Armies. We know that our Division Commander, General Taylor, will say: "Well Done!"

We are giving our country and our loved ones at home a worthy Christmas present and being privileged to take part in this gallant feat of arms are truly making for ourselves a Merry Christmas.

McAULIFFE,
Commanding.

A WAC Remembers the Lurline

By the end of 1943 nearly 60,000 women had joined the Women's Army Auxiliary Corps (WAAC), filling noncombat jobs. They received no official military rank, no pay for dependents, or many other benefits offered to the regular army. The problem was so acute that Congress passed a law during the war establishing the Women's Army Corps (WAC) to remove the auxiliary status and to provide greater rewards for women's service. So successful was that service that General Dwight D. Eisenhower remarked, "In some cases one WAC has been able— because of her expert training—to perform tasks that previously required two men. The smartness, neatness, and esprit constantly exhibited has been exemplary." Carolyn Comer of Oklahoma City was

★ 1944 ★

*On Christmas Eve
1944, a determined First
Lieutenant Phyllis
Hocking checks a GI's
glucose IV at the
Thirty-sixth Evacuation
Hospital, Palo, Leyte, in
the Philippines. The
hospital is quartered in
a church, and behind
nurse and patient, the
congregation kneels in
prayer. Almost 60,000
women served in the
Army Nurse Corps in
World War II. Sixteen
were killed in action
and 1,600 were
decorated for
meritorious service and
bravery. So great was
the need for their
services that in 1943 the
federal government
began to subsidize
nursing education. In
fact, in the spring of
1945, the supply of new
nurses was barely
enough to keep
Congress from
including them in the
military draft. The
quality of the Corps'
work can be seen in the
less than 4 percent
mortality rate for
wounded soldiers who
were reached in the
field or evacuated.*

★ ★ ★

*one of those WAC members. On board a converted luxury liner,
the **Lurline,** she spent a memorable Christmas in 1944.*

WHEN I JOINED the WAC during WW II, I was working for the Inspector of Naval Materials Office at Fisher Bodies, Pontiac, Michigan. Ensign Horst from Iowa was my boss. Lieutenant Harry C. Cox was our officer in charge.

Our headquarters was located in the Detroit Free Press Building in Detroit. That newspaper donated 10,000 decks of playing cards that were received by the "Lurline." On the way to New Guinea in December 1944, I worked in the ship's library in the evenings, and I gave out half of the playing cards to the GIs and WACs. I also played the piano in chapel. We all loved our ship's chaplain.

Members of the American Red Cross from all over the U.S. gave Christmas wrapped ditty bags of gifts to each passenger aboard the troop ship. They were marked "male" or "female." I wrote a letter to the Beaumont, Texas, newspaper and they printed it. Later a former WAC wrote to me that she had been married on the "Lurline" when she went to the Pacific. When she returned home she joined the Red

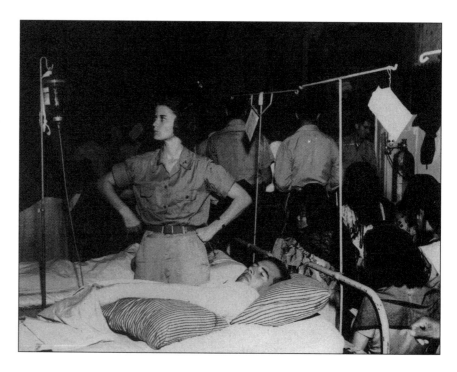

*Members of the all-black 6888th Postal Directory Unit parade in Rouen. These WACs had to face discrimination based on gender **and** race. The Women's Bureau of the U.S. Department of Labor declared after the war that most women did "women's work" in the service, such as typing and stenography. Commanded by Lieutenant Colonel Charity E. Adams, the 6888th was the only African-American unit of the segregated WACs to serve overseas. At its peak, the number of women in the military in World War II was about 270,000, of whom only about 4,000 were black. By far, most served in the WACs. Their Navy counterparts, the WAVEs, had fewer than 100, and the Coast Guard SPARs, even fewer. The WACs would not be fully integrated until 1951.* ☆ ☆ ☆

Cross and had helped to make many ditty bags—still being given to military personnel—the bags filled with gifts.

On that Christmas Eve, we went to bed and heard Santa Claus with sleigh bells coming to fill our stockings with cosmetics. We were delighted. Santa was our WAC officer, Lieutenant Booth.

We were told that the Japanese had bombed Biak, located on the Equator about 450 miles north of Hollandia, Dutch East Indies. It was reported that fifty-five GIs were killed and thirty-seven wounded while attending a theater.

Lieutenant General George C. Kenney, who rose to commander of the Allied Air Force of the Southwest Pacific, had an illustrious career in the war not only as a leader, but for his inventiveness for bombing techniques. He was from Oklahoma and was Adjutant General for the Oklahoma National Guard for many years—thirty years, I have heard.

Of Diaper Pins and Jellies

A war ration book, emblematic of shortages and sacrifice on the home front. In ordinary times, Americans associate Christmas with plenty—of food, travel, and gifts drawn from the world's most prolific production lines. But that expectation was sharply curtailed during World War II. The government halted the sale of new automobiles and tires because metal and rubber were needed for the war effort. All new-car production was halted in February. The factories that had been making cars were now going to become the producers of tanks, planes, and guns. There followed in the next few years restrictions on everything from butter to bicycles. The recently created Office of Price Administration (OPA) administered this rationing.

✦ ✦ ✦

War rationing affected the entire nation. Sugar, meat, coffee, fuel oil, rubber—all were rationed. In May 1942 the government limited individuals to four gallons of gasoline a week and lowered the national speed limit to forty miles per hour.

Many American factories were converted into war plants, and the production of new automobiles was discontinued in February 1942. One well-known ditty of the period proclaimed:

And when I die, please bury me
'Neath a ton of sugar, by a rubber tree.
Lay me to rest in an auto machine
And water my grave with gasoline.

Sensitive to the sacrifices of the populace, a writer for **Woman's Day** *had a Christmas suggestion for readers.*

CHRISTMAS SAVING

The urge to avoid using much-needed paper on Christmas gifts is stimulating quite a little prankishness on the part of the ingenious. One woman has decided to wrap all her baby presents in diapers and pin them up; another to wrap gifts of jams and jellies in a crisp new kitchen towel; anyone wishing to wrap our gift in a mink coat can save a lot of paper that way.

A generation earlier during World War I, in an astonishing Christmas story, German and British troops stopped fighting along a front in "No Man's Land," shared food, and even, some claim, played football. "Just you think," remembered one British soldier, "I was out talking and shaking hands with the very men I had been trying to kill a few hours before." The mystery writer Arthur Conan Doyle called this Christmas truce "an amazing spectacle . . . one human episode amid all the atrocities which have stained the memory of the war." Although no truces on such a grand scale were reported in World War II, Erroll Laborde's remembrance of his father's stories about Bastogne and the sounds of German soldiers caroling at night on Christmas suggest special feelings of humanity amid chaos and ruin.

MY FATHER USED TO TELL the stories about Christmas during the war. In 1944, he, along with a half-million other GIs and a force of British soldiers, were huddled in the snow in the Ardennes Forest, which sprawls across corners of France, Belgium, and Luxembourg. On the other side were 600,000 Germans preparing for what would be known as the Battle of the Bulge. During the struggle, which lasted from Dec. 16 to Jan. 28, soldiers spent the holiday at war while nearly being buried beneath banks of snow. The only Christmas decorations to come from this struggle were purple hearts. My father almost lost a leg that was nearly frozen during the siege. There was no joy to his world that winter, but even from the despair there was a special memory—German soldiers, in the distance, caroling at night.

He lived long enough to see most of the commemoration of the 50th anniversary of the war, although I regret that he did not have an opportunity to go back and walk the fields where he, a boy from rural Louisiana serving as a medic, saw the harsh realities of battle.

From his perspective, shivering in a foxhole, the warm glow of Christmas in Louisiana must have been a solar system away . . .

Nazi Germany had seen the Bulge as a last effort to try to salvage the war in its favor. It failed. With the allied victory, the war in Europe was almost over. German surrender was only a few months away.

I wish I could hear my father talk about that Christmas again, but at least he had opportunities to tell the story. Thousands of soldiers,

Was Christmas ever more reduced to the basics? Sergeant John F. O'Brien, in a foxhole in the Monscha area of Germany on December 23, 1944, a long way from his native Pittsburgh, celebrates Christmas by doing what he can with what he's got. In his mind's eye that bush may remind him of the Christmas tree back home. But it's not likely that the one in the living room in Pittsburgh was decorated with C ration cans or that his family tree bore tinsel that had been dropped from a plane, the way this tinsel was supplied. The photograph does tell us that it could have been a worse Christmas. There's obviously no one firing at him, because it's safe for him to stand up and pose for this picture.   ☆ ☆ ☆

fatalities from both sides, never would. War is hell. In a season perpetually in search of the right spiritual tone, those men should be remembered.

For those who survived, the holidays of the future must have been joyous by comparison. They would always remember that shivering, snow-packed winter in the Ardennes, while at the same time joining future generations in the chorus of those dreaming of a white Christmas.

In Prison; Conquering Despair

Pastor David Read spent several Christmas seasons of World War II in a prison camp in Bavaria. He says that today when he catches sight of a church invitation on a New York bus to "come home for Christmas," he rejoices in the "deeper meaning that could sustain us" even in the worst of circumstances.

RECENTLY, as I was fumbling through a drawer full of mementos of those war years, I came across a torn and crumpled bit of paper on which I recognized the opening lines of a poem I had written in the prison camp at Christmas 1944. They took me right back to that last prison Christmas. The cynics were having their day, and no one dared to say "Home by Christmas." The news might be good, but once again, as in the early days, we were desperately short of food, and increasingly aware (though we never spoke about it) that we were in the hands of an unpredictable maniac who was unlikely to let us go home in peace, whether at Christmas or any other time. And were these allied planes we saw and heard? Encouraging, yes, but did the pilots of our planes know the difference between a SS Headquarters and a POW camp?

All this had added up to a new slogan: "Let's not celebrate Christmas this year." No carols, no pageants, not even those astonishing recipes with which we concocted unbelievable Christmas puddings. The lost poem had been my response—and the response of all those who had kept the flicker of faith alive. The opening lines brought it all back:

> *"Let's not celebrate Christmas this year"?*
> *God, what a yelp from Christian men!*

This ad from Nash, a now long-gone automobile company, suggests what's on the mind of a typical soldier as the war's end seems close enough to touch. It's the thoughts, feelings, sights, and smells of home. But then he's jolted out of his reverie by the reality that still puts him in harm's way and places him far away from those he loves. Nash is trying to make the point that American business, too, is anticipating the end of the conflict, and is aware that it will have to be prepared to convert quickly back to civilian production to meet pent-up demand for automobiles. The company, in assuring the public that it "will contribute the jobs and wages that will keep this nation strong in peace as in war," is speaking to the memory of the recent Depression, vanquished, finally, only by the massive orders for war matériel.

☆ ☆ ☆

The point to the poem was simple and worth dwelling on, no matter what our circumstances. I remember asking if any could think of Peter, Paul and the other apostles writing of their confidence in the Gospel of Christ, but suggesting that there were occasions when they should give in to despair. Can we imagine any writer of an epistle to these first Christians saying "I know you are going through a very rough time, so why not forget about celebrating The Incarnation." Paul reminded his friends at Philippi that he had known imprisonment, floggings, shipwreck, starvation, but launched into a celebration of the Incarnation that still echoes in our hearts and minds (see Philippians 2:1–11).

We were not in special danger or deprivation when I wrote that poem; but a few miles away Dietrich Bonhoeffer, after months of trials and threats to his life, was in the hands of the Gestapo awaiting the scaffold which was prepared for him. I cannot imagine him writing one of his letters from prison complaining that this was no time for Christmas celebrations. His letters breathed a total confidence in his Savior.

The Gospel is no less true when circumstances are most terrible. If we soak ourselves in this truth we shall never find ourselves making excuses for our lack of desire to celebrate or offer any excuses to our flock. May Christmas joy be real and radiant for us all—no matter what our circumstances.

Home on Jackson Street

No one street in America during World War II could be called typical. And yet, across the country, the people of all American streets shared in the war struggle. All families were touched by the war, some through personal military service or the service of a relative, others through the effects of rationing and war production. In towns and cities throughout the country during Christmas 1944, many windows had more than wreaths and holly; they had gold and blue stars signifying soldiers from those homes, some of whom would never return. All Americans yearned for the time when the anxieties and fears would be lifted. Writers Adele Bernstein and Anne Hagner looked at Jackson Street, Washington, D.C.

THE ONE THOUSAND BLOCK of Jackson Street NE is as American as ham and eggs.

When you look down the block, the gray-barked maples and oaks, the small neat homes set back in hedged yards, the children and dogs playing in the street, the aproned mothers chatting across porches, all spell solid comfort—and home.

Christmas wreaths and holly frame many windows, an unusual number of packages are being delivered, and youngsters are excited. The Yuletide magic has cast its spell.

But there are thirteen blue stars and one gold one in the windows of the one thousand block of Jackson street. There are Red Cross stickers. A young soldier walks down the block and children hail him proudly.

Jackson Street is playing its part. The entire block thrills when a boy comes home on furlough. It is anxious when another is called. It mourns, genuinely, the boy who won't come back . . .

If there is complacency in the United States about the war, Jackson Street doesn't know about it. The folks on this little street, which is so quiet you don't bother to look for traffic, are so busy living, working, saving, hoping, praying, that they don't have time for anything else. The postman is the important man these days and a letter from overseas is apt to be read up and down the block—then back to the business of feeding the family with homemade vegetable soup, homemade mince pies, and pot pies. Jackson Street has the most delicious odors imaginable.

Men of the 303rd Bombardment Group receive Holy Communion on Christmas Day at an air base somewhere in England. The 303rd flew their first mission in November 1942, but they were stymied by bad weather that day and had to return without hitting their target, a submarine base in France. But in their next 362 missions, they earned their nickname, "Hell's Angels." Their honor role includes two Medal of Honor winners.

★ ★ ★

A Combat Medic on the Front Keeps in Touch

Early in 1942 the U.S. military devised a method to deliver pieces of news back and forth from home to servicemen overseas. It was called V-Mail, for victory. A simple photographic system, V-Mail used a one-sided form on which the writer composed the message. The message was then photographed onto 16mm black-and-white camera film, sent to a processing center on a reel containing many other letters, printed onto a piece of five-by-four-inch black-and-white photographic paper, folded, and slipped into an envelope for delivery. The mail system vied with food, fuel, ammunition, and other supplies for precious overseas cargo space; V-Mail allowed a massive exchange of personal messages, which otherwise could not have occurred. During the course of the war, over 1.5 billion V-Mail letters were processed. One of the V-Mail users was Keith Winston, citizen soldier serving in a medical battalion aid station in the Ardennes Forest siege during Christmas 1944. Keith kept in touch with his wife Sarah and their two sons.

At Christmas 1944, the Middle East, and all of North Africa to the west, was at peace, a condition that would prevail there for at least a few more years.

★ ★ ★

TODAY IS CHRISTMAS, and I'm feeling low, realizing today's significance when families are usually together. I hope you, in some way, enjoyed the day with the children.

Fortunately, not much "activity" and we had a rather restful day, and just about the best GI meal I ever had. A turkey drumstick. It must have weighed a pound—cranberry sauce, potatoes, peas, mince pie. I ate so much I just couldn't touch the pie.

And last night we had a little party. I was in charge of refreshments and everything went off pretty well. We pulled open the table, and about twice the size of our table . . . Through the center we ran a long sheet of tissue paper—toilet, to be exact—and on it we placed glasses for drinks. Candles were lit around a little Christmas tree in the center. We served salads of tuna, and sardines and crackers, bread, coffee.

Also pineapple and fruit cake. Then we sang carols and had a pleasant time. Some of the civilian neighbors were invited in and they sang "Silent Night" in German for us. We weren't kidding ourselves—despite the outward gaiety, we knew we were hiding our real feelings of home and kids and an American Christmas.

This morning we awoke at 6 A.M. to the whistling of Silent Night by our Sergeant, and it turned my thoughts to you—and being 6 hours ahead in time, I could picture you wrapping up packages for the boys, making last minute preparations—and it was a little tough for me to take.

Private Walter E. Przybyla of Chicopee, Massachusetts, and the Second Infantry Division could probably imagine warmer, cheerier, and more convenient places and circumstances in which to be addressing Christmas cards. That's the top of a box that serves as Private Przybyla's writing desk, and those are artillery shells at his elbow. His cards will reach his loved ones addressed from "somewhere in Germany." Security concerns prevented the GIs from giving an exact return address.

★ ★ ★

Lesson on a Blackboard

All along the front in the Ardennes, military units fought small skirmishes, sometimes at such close range that some of the 250,000 German soldiers assaulting the 83,000 American troops fell dead into American foxholes. Frostbitten and exhausted, the sides pounded each other with unrelenting tank and machine-gun firepower that left a devastating toll of killed and wounded. Most of the soldiers did not realize the scale of the total battle, assuming, as one soldier remembered, that "theirs was just a small counteroffensive." When it was over, one Belgian schoolteacher reentered his ruined classroom to find writing on the blackboard. The message was from a German soldier.

May the world never again live through such a Christmas night. Nothing is more horrible than meeting one's fate, far from mother, wife and children. Is it worthy of man's destiny to bereave a mother of her son, a wife of her husband, or children of their father? Life was bequeathed us in order that we might love and be considerate to one another. From the ruins, out of blood and death shall come forth a brotherly world.
(signed) a German officer. ★

Emerging from the Cellars

Many survivors of the Battle of the Bulge remember hearing German voices at the front singing "Silent Night." Lieutenant Charles Stockell, an artillery observer for the Second Division, was one who overheard. His company was holed up in a cellar, out of the cold and out of the way of enemy shelling. He remembered the firing dying down as midnight and Christmas Day approached.

AT THE STROKE OF MIDNIGHT, without an order or a request, dark figures emerged from the cellars. In the frosty gloom voices were raised in the old familiar Christmas carols. The heavy snowflakes fell softly, covering the weapons and signs of war. The infantry, in their front line positions, could hear voices two hundred yards away in the dark joining them, in German, in the words to "Silent Night." It was a time when all men could join the holy and sacred memories of the story of the Christ Child, and renew a fervent prayer for "peace, goodwill toward men!"

An African-American Musician's Prayer

While General George S. Patton was known for praying at the Battle of the Bulge on Christmas, he was not alone. First Lieutenant Benjamin Layton was another. A native of Hanover, Virginia, and a graduate in chemistry from Virginia Union University, Layton was also a musician and bandleader. By March 1942 he was part of an infantry officers' class at Fort Benning, Georgia; he was the only African-American in the class. In mid-December Layton arrived with his unit in Bastogne. A few days before Christmas Eve, his birthday, Layton's men, cut off from supply troops by treacherous weather and enemy forces, had nothing to eat but chocolate bars.

AFTER THE REMAINDER of his company arrived, Layton said, the weather "just started getting worse and worse."

. . . He said it wasn't long before his company began hauling troops and supplies to the front—and hauling bodies and pieces of bodies of American soldiers back.

He recalled trucking "green" troops of the Seventy-fifth Infantry Division to within five kilometers of the front. Layton said a colonel commanding one of the regiments told him that, of all the regiments in the entire army, his had the youngest overall age.

"Things had gotten so dreadful that mortar fire was falling all around. What really got me was taking these units up and bringing back parts of bodies—these youngsters—the cream of the crop," he said . . .

General George S. Patton's Third Army units had been ordered north to relieve the siege at Bastogne, but it was questionable whether or not they could make it in time.

"Everyone was saying it looked like we all would have to surrender or be killed, and everybody was saying it's impossible for Patton's army to come all that distance through this dreadful weather—without sleeping and without food . . . Things looked awfully bleak," he recalled.

Layton . . . called a number of his men together, and they thought he was preparing to recite his often-offered poem—"Snow," which he said his brother wrote in 1931 "at the height of the Depression" in Hanover, Virginia. Instead, he told them, "No, I'm not reciting the poem, I'm going to pray." With that, he said the strangest and one of the shortest prayers he'd ever said. "I just looked up and I said, 'God! God! Please let me celebrate my twenty-seventh birthday!'"

On Christmas Eve morning, his birthday, Layton was awakened by the roar of Allied-aircraft flying east to attack German positions. "We looked up in the sky, and the sky was filled with planes."

Although Patton had asked his chaplain to write a prayer for relief in the "intemperate" weather, Layton said his company told him, "Lieutenant, we know you are highly religious, but we didn't know that you had that much influence on God."

These servicemen and women are decorating a tree at the American Red Cross Club in Calcutta, India. African-Americans were segregated in Red Cross facilities during World War II, as elsewhere. Most black units were commanded by white officers. Their manual, which was classified, stated: "The officer will not be able to answer adequately all questions which Negro troops may ask concerning their relation to a democratic Army. But he can make certain that, within his own unit, the democratic principles which the Negro soldier has come to accept as an American ideal will operate." Although it was well into the war before blacks were allowed to see action on a fighting front, they fought with exceptional bravery. But of the 433 Medals of Honor awarded in World War II, blacks initially received none. Just a few years ago, seven African-Americans received the medal in a belated recognition of their valor.

★ ★ ★

Inside a Belgian Church

The snow might have been a pretty touch to the end of the holiday season if it hadn't been **inside** this church, in ruins in the Ardennes Forest of Belgium at the beginning of January. Late in the war, Belgium was suffering more than physical destruction as German armies made a last attempt to halt the Allied invasion of their homeland. Belgian partisans, who harassed German soldiers with everything from wrong directions to sniper fire, were being shot by the feared Gestapo, which accompanied the German troops. In the town of Bande, on December 24, the Gestapo shot more than thirty-five Belgian men, including several priests, dumping their bodies in a nearby cellar. Nor were American soldiers immune to such atrocities. In Malmedy, GIs were machine-gunned after they had already surrendered.

✦ ✦ ✦

125

Miracle on a Train

I ARRIVED AT THE San Diego railroad station early one 1944 morning and joined throngs of anxious holiday travelers who were burdened with baggage and Christmas gifts. We climbed aboard the overbooked holiday train. Lines of military and civilian passengers pushed and shoved each other, scrambling for the last remaining seats.

It would take an eternity—four days and four nights—to reach New York City. Still weak from malaria and hurting from my recent battle wounds, I was not looking forward to this long, boring trip.

I struggled down the aisle, carrying my Marine Corps seabag. Panic set in as I neared the end of the car. It was the last one, and all the seats looked occupied. My anxiety was interrupted by a loud voice: "Over here, Marine, and hurry up; I have a seat for you."

I hurried over, sat next to a sailor and thanked him for the seat.

"Hi, mate," he said. "They call me 'Ski,' because of my long Polish last name."

I replied, "Hi, mate. They call me 'Eddy Lee,' because of my long Ukrainian name."

We both grinned and clumsily shook left hands. My wounded right hand was in a sling; and his right arm was amputated, with his empty jumper sleeve pinned up at the shoulder.

When I saw the many Navy men and women struggling through the narrow aisle, I asked Ski why he, a Navy man, gave me, a Marine, this seat.

"Well, I saw your shoulder patch, your combat ribbons, and battle stars, and I knew that you and I fought in the same campaigns. You were on the land, and I was on the sea. I served aboard the USS *Chicago*, a cruiser named after my hometown. I lost my arm when we were torpedoed off the island you were fighting on."

The locomotive's loud steam whistle blew, then with the clang of its large bell we started to move, heading east across southern California.

Ski and I were both proud of the Navy and Marine Corps, but were bitter toward the military hospital we had just left. It had an inefficient administrative system and the medical staff was overworked and burned out. Four years of war and the continuous flow of casualties had created a callous attitude.

We were disenchanted with the negative treatment we had received

In four years as a marine, Edward Andrusko had been wounded three times. When he arrived at the San Diego railroad station at Christmastime 1944, he was recovering from his latest wound as well as a case of malaria. He was headed home to New York; it would take him four days and four nights to get there.

from the military and the apathetic civilian world since our return to the United States. It was this type of poor management that put rehabilitating servicemen on this crowded train rather than on an airplane.

This would be my fourth Christmas away from home, and the season always made me sad because of the many friends who had died in battle during this holiday.

Our train was traveling at maximum speed, but across the great American desert it seemed like we were not moving fast enough. We had too much time on our hands.

We could sleep sitting up in our seats, stand in line for meals and washroom, or reminisce bittersweet battle memories with our train mates. Ski and I agreed that we both became near atheists and cynics after three years of war. Soon we tried to sleep the time away.

En route to Denver, our train would wind ever so slowly through many tunnels, around picturesque snow-covered mountains and valleys. I consoled myself that time was no longer important. What was my hurry— I would miss Christmas at home by a day. My parents had split up, and I had no home to go to. My girlfriend of four years sent me a "Dear John" letter, saying she had waited too long for me to return and found someone else. And worst of all, when I was well enough for duty, I could be sent overseas to battle again.

We left Denver early in the morning in a snowstorm. Our train's whistle blew often as we charged across the prairie states through a howling blizzard. It was nightfall somewhere in Illinois. Our train slowed to a crawl because of poor visibility. It was freezing outside and getting colder inside our passenger coach on this Christmas Eve.

The train conductor entered our car and called out, "It's ten o'clock, two hours to Chicago, next stop Chicago!" He dimmed the lights and left.

Two soldiers of the Twenty-ninth Division of the Ninth Army bring a bit of Christmas cheer to an otherwise bleak entrance to their headquarters near the German border on December 15. At the beginning of January, the Ninth Army will join in an attack on the northern flank of the German advance into the Ardennes—the "Bulge"—and will prevail against an enemy short of reserves and feeling the strain on men and matériel from the devastating Russian attack coming from the east in Poland and East Prussia.

★ ★ ★

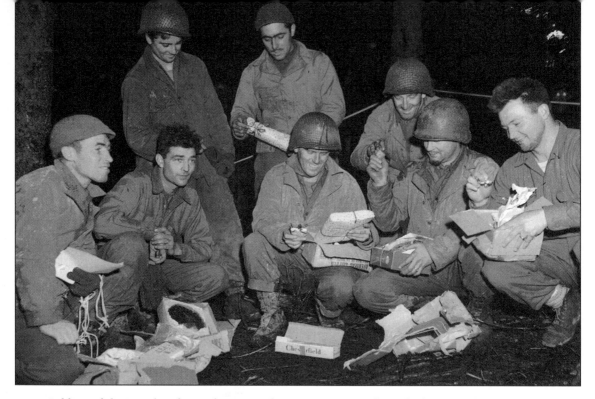

Soldiers of the Fourth Infantry, known as the "Ivy" Division (from the letters in the Roman numeral IV), open the first batch of their Christmas packages in the Hürtgen Forest, near Zweifall, Germany, on December 14. The Fourth Infantry Division was the first Allied unit to land on Utah Beach on D day, where Lieutenant Colonel Theodore Roosevelt, Jr., earned the Medal of Honor. They drove inland, took Cherbourg, and were, again, the first unit to enter Paris and, later, the first to cross into Germany. But at the Hürtgen Forest in November and early December, at the approach to the Ruhr Valley, they were bloodied by an enemy entrenched in the dark woods. There Lieutenant Colonel George L. Mabry won his Medal of Honor. Withdrawn from combat to recuperate, they are here two days away from again facing the attacking Germans, in the Battle of the Bulge.

✯ ✯ ✯

Ski turned to me and said, "Eddy Lee, I'm worried about my family meeting me at the Chicago station and seeing me like this. I asked my girl not to come. What should I do or say to them?"

"Act natural, they know about your arm, try to be yourself," I said. "You all love each other, and I'll bet they will thank God that you made it home alive. It will all work out fine; you'll see. Now let's try to get some sleep."

Our train suddenly made an unscheduled, metal-screeching stop. A few waking passengers muttered, "What's going on?" Most went back to sleep.

I looked out the window and could see only a small, dimly lighted railroad station surrounded by large snowdrifts. The door at the other end of the car opened, and in the darkened car, I could just barely see a small boy and a mature woman coming into our coach.

They walked slowly up the aisle, looking at the passengers, apparently looking for a seat. The two strangers cautiously headed toward my end of the car.

I closed my eyes and tried to get back to sleep, wondering why the train was not moving. It just sat there at this lonely, dark railroad station. I fell asleep for a few minutes, until I heard a noise in front of me. I slowly opened my eyes and saw the young boy, about eight or nine years old standing in front of me, staring.

The boy smiled and said, "Welcome home and a Merry Christmas, Marine. My grandmother and I would like to give you a gift and thank you for serving our country."

The boy handed me a dollar bill and then shook my hand. The grandmother put her arm around me and said, "God bless you." Then they both smiled and said, "Merry Christmas and good-bye."

I was surprised and moved. I said, "Thank you, thank you very much." I searched in my seabag for some sort of Christmas gift for the boy. When I looked up, they were gone.

Our train whistle blew; we lunged forward and were rolling again. I quickly looked out my frosty window and saw the boy and his grandmother leaving the dismal railroad station. I waved goodbye as they slipped into the darkness. They did not see me.

I sat back in my seat bewildered, wondering what had just happened. Had it been real? I queried Ski and the two soldiers sitting across from me if they too had seen the little boy and his grandmother. They said, "No, we were sleeping." Ski added, "You must have been dreaming."

My mind raced with questions. Who were they? Why did they pass by all those other servicemen, including other marines, and then stop in front of me? Maybe I was sleeping, and with all the medication I was taking for pain and malaria, it just could have been a strange, nice dream.

It was two more hours to Chicago, and I decided to try to get some sleep. But before closing my eyes, I looked down at my tightly closed fist. I slowly opened my hand and there was a crumpled-up dollar bill.

I contentedly fell asleep with my precious gift tucked safely in my pocket and a pleasant feeling in my heart, the nicest feeling I had in a very long time.

The conductor came into the car and announced our arrival in Chicago. Passengers took their baggage from the overhead compartments. I helped Ski with his seabag. He was getting off. He was home.

Ski and I said our emotional good-byes as the train came to a stop. The crowd of passengers left through both exit doors. I sat back, waiting to continue my odyssey of another thousand miles to New York City.

It was midnight. As I looked out the train window, I was surprised to see hundreds of people, young and old choirs of many ethnic and racial backgrounds on the station platform, all holding candles and sheet music and singing Christmas carols. The people and the station were all decked out with the holiday spirit and decorations. It was a bitterly cold, snowy Christmas night in Chicago, but the holiday spirit was cheerful and warmed all our hearts.

As I enjoyed the joyful singing, our train car doors opened and the singing choirs of young people paraded in. Each singer carried a tray of food and drinks. Each tray held a complete Christmas dinner with a small gift on it. There were enough trays for everyone on the train. We were no longer strangers. We all sang, ate and celebrated together. It

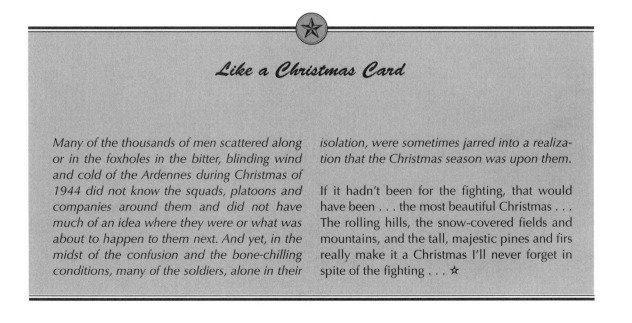

Like a Christmas Card

Many of the thousands of men scattered along or in the foxholes in the bitter, blinding wind and cold of the Ardennes during Christmas of 1944 did not know the squads, platoons and companies around them and did not have much of an idea where they were or what was about to happen to them next. And yet, in the midst of the confusion and the bone-chilling conditions, many of the soldiers, alone in their isolation, were sometimes jarred into a realization that the Christmas season was upon them.

If it hadn't been for the fighting, that would have been . . . the most beautiful Christmas . . . The rolling hills, the snow-covered fields and mountains, and the tall, majestic pines and firs really make it a Christmas I'll never forget in spite of the fighting . . . ★

was the most beautiful, festive Christmas I had ever had. Our generous Chicago hosts cheerfully wished us a "very Merry Christmas and a welcome home!"

This train odyssey and these unbelievably beautiful events changed my bitter feelings. I really felt I did make it home for Christmas.

Many years later, I told this story to my family at Christmas time. I pondered out loud, "Who was that little boy on the train, and why did he and his grandmother choose me? Why me?"

Our visiting young niece was playing on the floor with her Christmas toy.

She had quietly listened to my sentimental wartime story and replied, "I know."

We all looked at her and I said, "You know what?"

"I know who the little boy on the train was, and why he picked you. The little boy was God, and he chose you because you were very, very sad and disappointed with everyone and everything. He wanted to make you happy again and welcome you home—and he did."

And then I knew a Christmas miracle had happened to me when I needed it most, during the war, on that train and in Chicago.

An American POW, a Jewish Doctor, and a Japanese Commander

Richard Gordon had been one of the defenders of the Philippine province of Bataan in 1942. Plagued by disease, malnutrition, fatigue, and a lack of basic supplies, Filipinos and Americans had bravely but vainly attempted to fight off experienced Japanese attackers. In April 1942 they surrendered after the Japanese had broken through the last main line of resistance. Assembling their captives in various sectors of Bataan, the Japanese sent them off to various prison locations. What ensued has become known as the "Death March"—basically a fifty-five-mile trek from Mariveles, Bataan, to San Fernando, Pampanga. If the prisoners survived the heat, the beatings, and the torture, they were placed in train cars and sent to Capas, Tarlac, a distance of around twenty-four miles. Dozens died standing up in the packed, sweltering railroad cars. The survivors were marched another six miles to Camp

O'Donnell and perhaps on to other locations. Several thousand men died during this Death March. Richard Gordon survived. He spent three years in a POW camp in Japan. In 1944 he and his fellow prisoners decided to celebrate Christmas.

I<small>T WAS OUR LAST</small> C<small>HRISTMAS</small> in captivity. We had no idea of how we would ever live to see Christmas 1945. The Japanese had assured us that in the event of an invasion, we would all be put to death. We had no reason not to believe them, as we saw no other way for the war to end.

In 1944, however, we decided to celebrate Christmas, even if it were to be our last one. Our Jewish doctor, Alfred Weinstein, conducted carol singing and read passages from the Book concerning Christmas.

Impressed by our Christmas spirit, our Japanese camp commander, one Lt. Kubo, ordered the release of Red Cross packages that had been in a warehouse for over two years. Each prisoner on Christmas Eve received a full box of American food. What a treat! No one slept that night, but surely the spirit of Christmas was as prevalent in that camp as if we were free men. It is a Christmas I remember every Christmas.

This USO troop is sending holiday greetings from Italy in 1944, but by then it could have been from any one of the organization's 3,000 locations throughout the world. The USO came into being on February 4, 1941, at the request of President Roosevelt, who had asked groups such as the Salvation Army and the YMCA to put together an organization that would provide free and wholesome recreation to young men and women far from home. The all-volunteer USO quickly flourished, and by war's end, about half a million volunteers had provided dances, teas, and movies to service personnel.

★ ★ ★

Although the U.S. military during World War II didn't always take advantage of the talent and skills that its personnel brought with them from civilian life, it probably succeeded better at this task than the traditional grumbling of GIs would have one believe. One kind of specialty that was put to good use was the ability of artists to not only record the great events of the day—and in World War II they happened just about every day—but also to capture the mood of these fateful years. Perhaps no other subject cried out more for artistic interpretation than the juxtaposition of wartime carnage with the celebration of Christmas.

LEFT. In "Silent Night," Coast Guard artist Ken P. Riley, Specialist Second Class, of Parsons, Kansas, depicts the Star of Bethlehem as a backdrop to a moment when a Coast Guardsman has made the ultimate sacrifice for peace. Riley was a veteran of three major South Pacific invasions.

ABOVE. Combat artist John Gretzer, Specialist Second Class, from Council Bluffs, Iowa, also places the Christmas star in the background, this time to a joyous—although also somewhat melancholy—scene of four shipmates joining in a carol somewhere in the cold North Atlantic. Gretzer had seen three European theater invasions firsthand.

☆ ☆ ☆

Death of a Pilot

For Mary Hilbert
and her parents, the
Christmas of 1944
approached with
gloom. A few months
earlier, in the skies
over New Guinea,
Mary's brother Bob
had perished in a tor-
pedo bombing raid.
In August, the Seattle
family had received
the never-forgotten
telegram, Bob's per-
sonal possessions, a
plat of his Philippines
burial site, and the
Distinguished Flying
Cross medal. They
were soon to receive
another package.

WE DREADED CHRISTMAS that year. It was 1944, and the war would never be over for our family.

The telegram had arrived in August. Bob's few personal possessions, the flag from his coffin, the plat of his burial site in the Philippines, [and] a Distinguished Flying Cross had arrived one by one, adding to our agonizing grief.

Born on a midwestern prairie, my brother rode horseback to school but wanted to fly an airplane from the first day he saw one. By the time he was twenty-one, we were living in Seattle. When World War II broke out, Bob headed for the nearest recruitment office. Slightly built, skinny like his father, he was ten pounds underweight.

Undaunted, he persuaded Mother to cook every fattening food she could think of. He ate before meals, between meals and after meals. We laughed and called him Lardo.

He stepped on the scale, still three pounds to go. He was desperate. His friends were leaving one after the other; his best buddy was already in the Marine Air Corps. The next morning, he consumed a pound of greasy bacon, six eggs, five bananas, two gallons of milk and, bloated like a pig, staggered back on the scale. He passed the weigh-in with eight ounces to spare.

When he was named Hot Pilot of primary training school in Pasco, Wash., and later involuntarily joined the "Caterpillar Club" (engine failure causing the bailout) at St. Mary's, California, we shook our heads and worried. Mother prayed. Bob was born fearless, and she knew it. Before graduating, he applied for a transfer to the Marine Air Corps at Pensacola, Fla. He trained in torpedo bombers before being sent overseas.

They said Bob died under enemy fire over New Guinea in the plane he wanted so desperately to fly.

Mother's faith sustained her, but my father aged before our eyes. He would listen politely when the minister came to call, but we knew Daddy was bitter. He dragged himself to work every day but lost interest in everything else, including his beloved Masonic Club. He'd wanted a Masonic ring real bad, and at Mother's insistence, he'd started saving for the ring, but that, too, ceased.

I dreaded the approach of Christmas. Bob had loved Christmas. His surprises were legendary: a doll house made at school, a puppy hidden in a mysterious place for our little brother, an expensive dress for Mother bought with the very first money he ever earned. Everything had to be a surprise.

What would Christmas be without Bob? Not much. Aunts, uncles and Grandmother were coming, so we went through the motions as much for memory as anything, but our hearts weren't in it.

On December 23, another official-looking package arrived. My father watched stone-faced as Mother unpacked Bob's dress blues. Silence hung heavy. As she refolded the uniform to put it away, a

A glorious Pacific sunrise creates a terrible beauty in this scene of a Coast Guardsman standing silently, reverently, in front of a grave of a fallen comrade. The crosses mark the final resting place of American soldiers who gave their lives to wrest a small atoll from the Japanese on the path to the Philippines. In 1944, when this picture was taken, that path would lead through major islands and some places that were barely spits of land in the vast Pacific. They had names such as Roi, Kwajalein, Eniwetok, Hollandia, Guam, and Morotai. At home Americans followed on maps the progress of soldiers, sailors, and especially the Marines, who were the first to hit the beaches and who took awful casualties. They triumphed, but so many paid the ultimate price.

★ ★ ★

mother's practicality surfaced, and she went through the pockets almost by rote.

In a small inside jacket pocket was a neatly folded $50 bill with a tiny note in Bob's familiar handwriting: "For Dad's Masonic ring."

If I live to be one hundred, I will never forget the look on my father's face. Some kind of transformation took place—a touch of wonder, a hint of joy, a quiet serenity that was glorious to behold. Oh, the healing power of love! He stood transfixed, staring at the note and the trimly folded bill in his hand for what seemed an eternity, then walked to Bob's picture hanging prominently on the wall and solemnly saluted.

"Merry Christmas, son," he murmured, and turned to welcome Christmas.

★ ★ ★

German prisoners of war in Pennsylvania take a break from work for a hot meal. The caption released with this photograph asserts that "treatment of internees is in strict accordance with the Geneva Convention." Ordinarily, when a government releases a publicity photo, it aims to get for it the widest distribution possible. But not when it's part of psychological warfare. With the war winding down and enemy morale clearly on the wane, the United States was suggesting that giving up was not the worst thing, and what better way to encourage it than to project an image of a beneficent captor? But the picture was not to be published in Allied countries, and was especially to be kept from American soldiers, who might not like the line that said that "the prisoners receive the same quality and quantity of food as is supplied to the U.S. armed forces."

In warfare, anything that can exploit the enemy's vulnerabilities is a weapon. These German leaflets aim to use Christmas as a weapon to prey upon Allied soldiers' weariness with war and longing for hearth and home and everything good suggested by the coming of Christmas.

★ ★ ★

The President Speaks to a Weary Nation

For the fourth year in a row, President Roosevelt addressed a nation at war. With his family and friends at the Roosevelt Hyde Park home for Christmas Eve, the President sat at the radio microphone and continued to rally the American people behind the war, the administration, and each other. A blend of the religious, political, and patriotic, the President's appeal was to carry on until the cause of freedom, peace, and Christmas would be realized.

It is not easy to say "Merry Christmas" to you, my fellow Americans, in this time of destructive war. Nor can I say "Merry Christmas" lightly tonight to our armed forces at their battle stations all over the world—or to our Allies who fight by their side.

Here, at home, we will celebrate this Christmas Day in our traditional American way—because of its deep spiritual meaning to us; because the teachings of Christ are fundamental in our lives; and because we want our youngest generation to grow up knowing the significance of this tradition and the story of the coming of the immortal Prince of Peace and Good-Will. But, in perhaps every home in the United States, sad and anxious thoughts will be continually with the millions of our loved ones who are suffering hardships and misery, and who are risking their very lives to preserve for us and for all mankind the fruits of His teachings and the foundations of civilization itself.

☆ ☆ ☆

LEFT. No government can manage the day-to-day tone of a relationship between two people, but in World War II it was in the national interest that men fighting overseas be confident of the continuity of love and affection from that special person back in the States. Morale was a weapon; neglect of a fighting man was akin to weakening American resolve. Many movie plots hinged on the GI who stands around at mail call only to be told, "Nothing today." Worse, a standard element in films and novels of the time was the "Dear John" letter, in which the girl back home got tired of waiting and went off and married someone else, plunging her former soldier beau into despair. The widely displayed government poster pictured here was a call to women on the home front to do their patriotic duty and write to their man.

★ ★ ★

Three members of the 163rd Engineers, from Philadelphia, Pennsylvania; Yonkers, New York; and Cumming, Georgia, pause on the German border to decorate a Christmas tree with ration cans. It's been more than six months and countless bloody miles since the Normandy invasion, and no one knows more than these men how much lies ahead in the invasion of Germany itself before they might be able to celebrate a more comfortable Christmas. They're responsible for building roads and bridges, laying and clearing minefields, building or blowing up fortifications, and constructing tank traps so that the rest of the Army can advance or defend itself. Their skills have been especially important in the still-raging Battle of the Bulge—with its emphasis on mobile warfare—in which the challenge has been to stop the onslaught of German tanks.

The Christmas spirit lives tonight in the bitter cold of the front lines in Europe and in the heat of the jungles and swamps of Burma and the Pacific islands. Even the roar of our bombers and fighters in the air and the guns of our ships at sea will not drown out the messages of Christmas which come to the hearts of our fighting men. The thoughts of those men tonight will turn to us here at home around our Christmas trees, surrounded by our children and grandchildren and their Christmas stockings and gifts—just as our own thoughts go out to them, tonight and every night, in their distant places.

We all know how anxious they are to be home with us, and they know how anxious we are to have them—and how determined every one of us is to make their day of home-coming as early as possible. And—above all—they know the determination of all right thinking people and nations, that Christmases such as those that we have known in these years of world tragedy shall not come again to beset the souls of the children of God.

This generation has passed through many recent years of deep dark-

ness, watching the spread of the poison of Hitlerism and fascism in Europe—the growth of imperialism and militarism in Japan—and the final clash of war all over the world. Then came the dark days of the fall of France, and the ruthless bombing of England, and the desperate battle of the Atlantic, and of Pearl Harbor and Corregidor and Singapore.

Since then the prayers of good men and women and children the world over have been answered. The tide of battle has turned, slowly but inexorably, against those who sought to destroy civilization.

And so, on this Christmas Day, we cannot yet say when our victory will come. Our enemies still fight fanatically. They still have reserves of men and military power. But, they themselves know that they and their evil works are doomed. We may hasten the day of their doom if we here at home continue to do our full share.

And we pray that day may come soon. We pray that until then, God will protect our gallant men and women in the uniforms of the United Nations—that He will receive into His infinite grace those who make their supreme sacrifice in the cause of righteousness, in the cause of love of Him and His teachings.

We pray that with victory will come a new day of peace on earth in which all the nations of the earth will join together for all time. That is the spirit of Christmas, the holy day. May that spirit live and grow throughout the world in all the years to come.

Barnacle Bill in the Admiralty Islands

Landing craft infantry (LCI) ships were designed to deliver assault troops quickly to the beaches. Each of the ships carried about 200 soldiers, who stormed onto the shores from ramps on each side of the craft. As one infantryman remarked: "Infantrymen cannot travel without the other services, and the final few thousand yards are the most difficult and harrowing." Although not designed for cross-ocean travel, many made trips from the United States to the Pacific theaters. They were flat-bottomed, extremely uncomfortable, relatively unprotected, but effective. Lewis Mason of the Landing Craft Infantry (G) 407 remembered the innovative ways in which he and his mates celebrated Christmas.

Few things are more poignant than World War II Christmas images of children displaced or orphaned by the conflict. This picture shows Santa at an American bomber base looking through Christmas cards that have been made by English children for English orphans and French evacuees, as the young recipients look on. Many English children lost their parents in the Blitz, the indiscriminate bombing that Luftwaffe head Hermann Göring hoped would break English morale. The Battle of Britain, which lasted a year beginning in mid-1940, killed as many as 600 civilians a day. Much of France was occupied by Germany in 1940, with a part of the country, nominally independent and ruled from Vichy, actually under German domination.

✮ ✮ ✮

Ahoy Mates! Christmas 1944 was an interesting one for the Crew of Landing Craft Infantry (G) 407. We were in the Admiralty Islands preparing to go to the Philippines for the Invasion of Lingayen Gulf on the island of Luzon. The Skipper had declared Holliday [*sic*] Routine for the Crew. We had Christmas dinner of canned turkey and something that Ship's Cook Fred Allen called dressing. All hands assembled on the forward Gun Deck to watch a skit that two of our crew members dreamed up. Karl Nyman and Bill Jim Hood pantomimed the Old Navy Song called Barnacle Bill the Sailor. Hood used helmet liners for breasts, a dress that he found in the rag bag, and a wig made from a mop. He played the fair young maiden. Nyman played Barnacle Bill to great success. I would say that this was the most interesting holiday that I spent during the war.

In the English Channel on Christmas Eve 1944, the Belgian troopship **Leopoldville** moved toward Cherbourg, France. Its mission—to transport over two thousand American soldiers to reinforce Allied troops at the Battle of the Bulge. About five and one half miles from its destination, the ship received a lethal torpedo blast from a German submarine. Within two and a half hours, the ship was under water. Hampered by delayed radio transmissions, heavy seas, freezing weather, an unprepared crew, and a lack of rescue equipment, the dimensions of the tragedy became greater with each passing minute. Plunged into the icy waters, hundreds of soldiers drowned; others froze to death. By the end of the night, nearly eight hundred Americans had lost their lives. It was the worst catastrophe ever to hit an American infantry division as a result of an enemy submarine attack.

Patton and Weather and God

Lieutenant General George S. Patton was speaking a lot to God lately. In November in Lorraine, with unrelenting rain plaguing his troops, Patton called Third Army chaplain Colonel James O'Neill and asked whether he had a prayer for relief. O'Neill complied. "Grant us fair weather for Battle," the prayer read, "Graciously harken to us as soldiers who call upon thee that, armed with Thy power, we may advance from victory to victory, and crush the oppression and wickedness of our enemies . . ." And now, as Patton's troops fought through horrible conditions in an attempt to rescue Bastogne's defenders, he issued a Christmas prayer to his troops. As Christmas Day dawned, the general jotted down in his diary: "A clear, cold Christmas, lovely weather for killing Germans, which seems a bit queer, seeing Whose birthday it is."

To each officer and soldier in the Third United States Army, I wish a Merry Christmas. I have full confidence in your courage, devotion to duty, and skill in battle. We march in our might to complete victory. May God's blessing rest upon each of you on this Christmas Day.

G.S. Patton
Lieutenant General
Commanding, Third United States Army ★

In the immediate aftermath of the disaster and the realization of the embarrassment that the loss of lives would mean to the Allied effort, the media was not informed of the sinking; even the relatives of the victims were not notified immediately. It was not until half a century later that the British government declassified documents relating to the **Leopoldville.** *On that ship that night was Private Edward Benson of Camden, New Jersey. His sweetheart, Margaret Mass, recalled the days following.*

We met in a skating rink. He was a clean living Christian, while I was a sophisticated New Yorker. Eddy planned to become a minister when he came back. Thinking I might become a minister's wife, I went to a Bible college in New York.

One evening I received a long-distance call from his father in Camden saying that Eddy was missing in action. It was then that I promised God I would finish what he started by going out as a missionary. And it was then that I realized that the two dozen roses I received by cable two weeks after Christmas were flowers from a dead man. Every time I rode the subway I was reminded of his habit of standing in the alcove at the end of the car with me and singing love songs to me above the roar of the train. We got engaged one night atop the Empire State building while looking down on twinkling Manhattan.

One of his buddies wrote me afterwards that he was up on deck with them singing Christmas carols but went down below to get his Bible. I guess he got stuck below deck.

"Wisht somebody would tell **me** *there's a Santa Claus."*

★ ★ ★
Willie and Joe's Christmas
To Willie and Joe, the haggard, wisecracking foot soldiers portrayed by cartoonist Bill Mauldin, the war was not heroic or ennobling. Caught up in the dreary disarray of life on the front, the two sullen dogfaces, shoulders bent, survived with grit and a sardonic sense of humor. To Willie and Joe, Christmas 1944 was another day to be endured. Writing for the GI publication **Stars and Stripes,** *Bill Mauldin won a Pulitzer prize in 1945 at the age of twenty-three.*

Fog, the Flying Fortress, and Christmas Eve

A. Willard "Hap" Reese flew B-17s, better known as "The Flying Fortresses" or "The Big Birds." They called Reese's 457th Bomb Group, which was part of the Eighth Air Force, "The Fireball Outfit." Reese and his fellow officers and crew look back on the "Forts" with a nostalgia and friendliness that belie the dangers they were in at the time, especially on this particularly unique Christmas Eve.

IT WAS THE MIDDLE OF DECEMBER in 1944 and the weather over Europe and England had been the worst in memory. Fog, rain and heavy overcast had shrouded the continent for many days. The Germans had broken through the Allied lines at the "Bulge," fighting was heavy at Malmedy [Belgium], and German tanks and troops were moving toward Antwerp unobstructed by fighters or bombers.

The Allied Air Forces had been grounded by the terrible weather for almost a week. It was a frustrating period. The Eighth Air Force had

☆ ☆ ☆

This youngster will just have to wait a moment for some attention from his soldier dad, who is otherwise occupied with embracing his wife. The soldier is one of those fortunate enough to get home for a Christmas reunion, and as a popular song of the day put it, "It's been a long, long time." Leave time, with its heady rush of longing suddenly fulfilled, was a constant theme in the music, movies, and popular fiction of the World War II era. In fact, on December 28, 1944, within a few days of the taking of this photo, **On the Town,** *a musical about sailors with just twenty-four hours of leave during which to see New York City, opened on Broadway.*

With Christmas coming on, these soldiers can be induced to smile while peeling potatoes in the city of Metz, in northeastern France near the German border. (That's a reasonable facsimile of a Christmas tree on top of the rotary sink.)

☆ ☆ ☆

been grounded at a time when the fate of the Allied invasion of the continent was at stake. Then, on December 23, we were alerted that the weather was expected to clear the next day. In anticipation of clear weather the Air Force Command ordered a "maximum effort" for Christmas Eve. A "maximum effort" required that every available plane in England was to be loaded with fuel, ammunition, and bombs and was to proceed to a designated target on the Continent.

According to official records of the Eighth Bomber Command, this December 24th raid was the largest air strike of WWII with 2034 bombers and 853 fighters. Until this mission the largest number of planes that had flown on a single mission from Glatton [England] was thirty-six. On this date the 457th Bomb Group was prepared to put up forty-five planes.

We were awakened very early on the morning of the twenty-fourth and through the darkness before dawn we could see that the weather was anything but clear. A cold rain mixed with snow was falling through a light fog. We could anticipate that by dawn this fog would become very dense . . . similar to other fogs that were familiar to those of us who had spent the past few months in England. Walking toward the ready room, hardly able to see ten feet ahead, we fully expected there would be no mission on this day. Instead, our flight positions were assigned, the target described, and the briefing proceeded in the usual manner. The target for the 457th was to be Koblentz [*sic*], Germany—a rail intersection that was very important for marshaling trains supplying German troops that were fighting in the Bulge.

As we proceeded through the fog by truck to our plane, loaded with flight gear, maps, flak vests, etc., we still fully expected a stand down. In violation of the order to maintain radio silence, the signal to taxi came by radio instead of by flare. The fog was too thick for us to be able to see the usual flares. As we taxied out, nose-to-tail, it was impossible to see anything except the plane that we were following. Takeoff was delayed again and again and it was nearing 10:00 A.M. when the word came by radio to commence takeoff.

We had been flying squadron, group, and deputy leads for the past 10 missions. It was the usual procedure to have the lead ships takeoff before any of the rest. Each of the lead ships carried radar units (sometimes referred to as a "Mickey" unit) that replaced the ball turret. We were the sixth plane in order of takeoff.

The other five lead planes ahead of us roared down the runway and were swallowed up in the fog before they had gone a hundred feet. When our turn came, we pulled out into position for takeoff and lined up on the runway centerline marker—we were unable to see the edges of the runway through the fog. The usual method of visually releasing a plane for takeoff was by flashing a green light from a small portable trailer stationed very near the edge of the runway at the point where we started our takeoff. We could not see the trailer through the fog.

A green light appeared from nowhere out of the fog. Did they really intend for us to take off under these conditions with a full fuel and bomb load? I called the tower to confirm (breaking radio silence) and told them I could not see the edge of the runway and could not reliably set my gyro compass. The response was "line up using your magnetic compass."

Well, we had practiced this in training but always considered it somewhat of a gruesome joke. For those of you familiar with a magnetic compass you know that it's like a cork in water and at best "comes close." True to our training, we did as we were ordered. We lined up magnetically and set the gyro as best we could. We locked the tail wheel, lowered the flaps to about half, set the turbo, checked the compass one last time and gave it full throttle—holding on the brakes as long as we could. Then we released and we were on our way.

Under these circumstances it was standard procedure for the bombardier to try to guide the pilot down the runway since the bombardier had the best view of the runway ahead. I listened intently for his familiar voice but heard nothing until—"We're going off." To me that meant he could see the edge of the runway and that we were about to leave the paved surface and encroach on the soft muddy grass field. I could not correct direction because I did not know whether we were going off to

Army Nurse Corps First Lieutenant Neva Rohar gives a Hershey bar from her Christmas box to a patient at the Ninety-fourth Evacuation Hospital, U.S. Ninth Army, Valkenburg, Holland, on December 15. Next to cigarettes, the Hershey bar was probably the closest thing to an all-purpose gift, survival food, and even informal currency in World War II. GIs trudging through war-battered Europe made instant friends of local children by giving them the gift of chocolate. And in the emergency rations carried by paratroopers dropping behind enemy lines just before D day, were four Hershey bars.

★ ★ ★

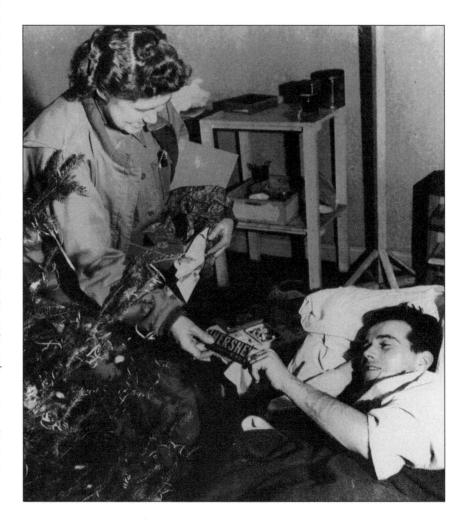

the left or to the right. If we left the runway, and the wheels were to dig into the mud at that speed, we were sure to nose over, and, with a full gas and bomb load we could expect a quick end to our tour.

A quick glimpse at the airspeed indicator showed our ground speed slightly over seventy mph (ninety mph is considered stalling speed). At this point I made the decision that we had no choice but to attempt to get airborne. With one quick motion and without taking my eyes off the instruments, I reached for the turbocharger and turned it clockwise as far as it would go. The engines literally screamed as the extra manifold pressure was applied to them.

We had been cautioned never to go to maximum manifold pressure except in extreme emergencies since this could easily blow a cylinder with ensuing disastrous consequences. Fortunately, that did not happen on this occasion. I pulled the stick back and it came quickly into my lap with almost no resistance at all.

As we slowly mushed off the runway at about eighty mph my mind flashed to the muddy field approaching and thoughts of the consequences if we could not stay airborne. At that instant we hit the soft earth—but with one bounce were again airborne. We raised our landing gear and began to pick up speed, flying completely on instruments. We seemed lost in a sea of fog for about two minutes more and then suddenly broke through the fog at about two hundred feet. Only a pilot who has experienced the thrill of suddenly breaking from a cloud into the clear atmosphere and blue sky can possibly know the feeling—and especially under these circumstances.

The fog lay like a blanket over England as far as one could see and above the fog was a crystal clear blue sky—beautiful flying weather. We had survived a takeoff that none of us would ever forget. Most of the members of our crew were unaware of how close we came to ending our tour—not over Germany, but on our home field.

As we began to climb above the fog, the waist gunner called on the intercom and noted that smoke was spiraling up from just under the area that we had broken through the fog. The ship that took off directly ahead of us had crashed.

We received word by radio from our field that all flights were scrubbed and no more planes would take off until the weather had cleared. The book "Fait Accompli," a history of the 457th, states that the last plane to take off crashed but it was actually the plane ahead of us. We were the last to take off.

An American soldier sits by a Christmas tree in Alsace, in the border area between France and Germany, on December 5, while a French grandmother mends his torn jacket. The placid scene belies the impending violence that is about to descend on the region. The German attack in the Ardennes, in Belgium, to the north, on December 16 will draw away American troops from this area. When the Battle of the Bulge begins to peter out at the end of the month, Germany will launch a second New Year's offensive here on December 31, hoping to capture Strasbourg, pull the American force back to the south, and cut American supply lines, enabling the Germans to resume their drive through the Ardennes toward the port of Antwerp. But the operation, dubbed North Wind, will fail.   ★ ★ ★

Here we were, five lead ships with no ball turret guns, representing the 457th bomb group, circling and climbing into formation. Orders came from the ground to "Proceed on the mission as scheduled." Six ball turret-less bombers on to Germany. Our group was apparently the only group assigned to bomb Koblenz, so, in keeping with the traditions of the Eighth, we carried on.

Hours later, with hundreds of planes in the bomber stream around us, we left the Division formation and turned toward our target. Noting our vulnerability, the group commander contacted fighter support and five P51's appeared just above our small formation criss-crossing over us. What a great sight to see our "Little Friends" giving us a personal escort.

On our approach to Koblenz we were spotted by a single ME-262 twin engine jet fighter. It was our first view of the new German jet. The pilot of the jet managed to stay just out of range of our 50 caliber guns, and, for the next 30 minutes, made numerous passes at us firing his 30 mm cannon shells into our formation. It appeared he was trying to draw off the fighters. The P-51's, wise to this maneuver, would chase him for a mile or two and then return to escort us. None of our planes were lost. Except for moderate flak at the target, the bomb run was uneventful. We later joined with another group and returned in loose formation to England.

Because we were so late getting started that morning, it was almost dark when we spotted the coast of England. To our dismay, the fog still covered our field and most of East Anglia. Radio reports told us that there were a few fields open east of London, so we proceeded to an English field near London and landed safely—the only time we used our landing lights since joining the 8th Air Force.

On Christmas Eve, General George S. Patton paused to record his thoughts in his diary. (Even generals can have trouble with German place-names; witness Patton's correction at the top of the page.) Here he drew up a balance sheet of where things stood between the Allies and the Germans with respect to men and matériel. Although a brave and successful general, Patton's difficulty with authority often got him in trouble and probably limited a career that might have been even more illustrious. In 1970, George C. Scott made the most of this fascinating personality in the Oscar-winning film **Patton.**

☆ ☆ ☆

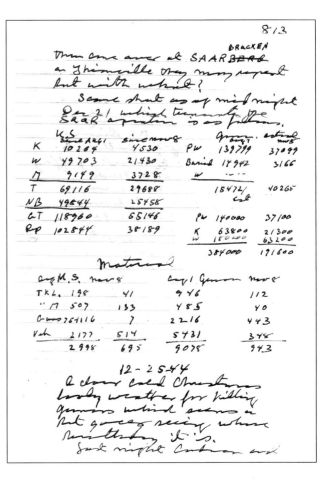

Landing at this field was yet another unexpected experience. Hundreds of other B-17's and B-24's, like us, had been forced to land at this field because of the weather. The field was solid with planes. When we touched down in the darkness, we could see planes parked just off our wing tips on both sides the full length of the runway. Almost every square inch of that field was covered with planes. I thought at that moment what damage a few Luftwaffe bombers could have done had they known.

This was Christmas Eve, 1944. We were an American flight crew far from home on a strange British airfield—but we were not alone. I remember singing Christmas carols with hundreds of other crew members around a Christmas tree in the mess hall. We slept on the floor that night, weary from the day's adventures, and returned to Glatton on Christmas day.

This is my memory of a Christmas Eve in 1944.

A Renewed Commitment

When Robert Alvey of the Eighty-third Infantry Division in Europe received this letter from his wife, Evelyn, they had been married for eleven years. The Carlsbad, California, soldier would carry the letter, along with his new ring, throughout the remainder of the war.

Dearest Honey:

This will be your Christmas letter. If you get it before Christmas (as you should, if the mail isn't held up) save it, and read it again on Christmas Day.

First of all, I looked all over town for a card to send with this ring. But none of them were good enough—some said "Merry Christmas," and that isn't what I want to say; some said "I love you," and while I want to say that, there are lots of other things I want to say, too. I decided I could write it better than any store-bought card could tell you. At least I can try.

I hope you like the ring and that it fits you, honey. Oh, God, how I wish I could put it on your finger! If it doesn't fit, send it back and try to send me your correct size somehow, and I'll have it fixed . . .

Christmas, 1944, won't be a merry one, honey; but it will be a loving one. It won't be a happy one, either. I can't be happy without you. But I shan't be too unhappy if I have some recent mail from you, and you are all right.

As for you, dear, I hope all of your packages get there before

Letters from home, especially at the holidays, provided a kind of reality check. For besides being hell, without those letters war entirely replaces one reality with another. On the battlefield, paranoia is often a sign of mental health. Dirt is normal, and it is everywhere; coarseness is part of everyday demeanor; and a little callousness is a shell that helps keep one whole. Without it, a soldier couldn't go on in the midst of grief over buddies dying all around him. These are survival skills to fit an extreme situation, but in the long run they are not life skills. So if this GI is ever to go back to "normal" life, he needs to hear about the church bake sale, who won the big high school football game, and what clever trick the family dog has learned now. For him, that is a true Christmas gift. ☆ ☆ ☆

Christmas; I hope you have a decent place to sleep, and decent food to eat; and don't be too lonely dear.

Remember that this is positively our first and last Christmas that we aren't going to be together. Think of all we have had, and just think of all we have to look forward to—years of happiness, and each year better than the last.

With this ring, honey, I want to renew the promises I made September 15, 1933—to love you and to cherish you forever.

Your devoted wife, Evelyn

Refugees

Belgian refugees make their way through Bastogne on December 30 after the 101st Airborne successfully held out against the Germans, a reminder that as hard as it is to be a soldier far from home at Christmastime, **losing** one's home and becoming a displaced person at the holidays is also very grim. In both World Wars I and II, Belgium had declared its neutrality. Nevertheless, each time it was overrun by Germany. In this conflict the invasion came on May 10, 1940, when the Netherlands and Luxembourg were also attacked. Belgium held out for less than three weeks, but was able to fight long enough to allow British troops to evacuate at Dunkirk. Four months after landing in Normandy in 1944, the Allies crossed into Belgium on September 3, and by February 1945 the country could begin the task of rebuilding.

✷ ✷ ✷

On Christmas Day, men of the XI Corps clearly appreciate the Christmas tree put up by their headquarters at Telegrafo on the island of Leyte in the Philippines.

✭ ✭ ✭

Meanwhile, a Santa Claus, wearing GI combat boots, brings Christmas to the children of Leyte. The scene of warmth and sweetness was bought at a terrible price, but now, late in the war, the Japanese have paid for it. The Allies reestablished this beachhead in the Philippines as a result of what historian Admiral Samuel E. Morrison called "the greatest naval battle of all time." The battle of Leyte Gulf engaged virtually the entire remnant of the Imperial Japanese Navy in what were really four battles, from October 20 to October 26. By the time the Japanese sailed away, they had lost twenty-six ships, while the Americans had lost seven. As Japanese historian Masonori put it, it was "complete revenge for Pearl Harbor."

✭ ✭ ✭

Jim Koerner of Kenilworth, New Jersey, was an engineer in the Tenth Armored Division. When interviewed after the war, Koerner, a man who had spent four and a half years in the service, been imprisoned in a German slave labor camp, and been beaten and nearly starved (he weighed less than one hundred pounds at the end of the war), said that he felt like an altar boy trying to talk to the pope when he met some of the other veterans who had gone through much more than he. But the supreme example of courage he witnessed came, he said, not from the fighting men but from a chaplain.

. . . THE BRAVEST MAN I ever met in my life was that priest from the 101st. That's why I was so attached to the 101st, because that priest, on Christmas Eve of 1944, they had us unloading ammunition. Wounded or not, you'll do it. We were throwing them shells hoping they'd blow them all to hell, I mean it. And they said, "You dumb bunch of sons . . ." get smacked with a gun. When he came along he had ten wounded paratroopers, and they told me right out, they said he had a chance to get back, and he said "I'm going with the men." Well, this is something that for ten years I couldn't talk. On Christmas Eve of '44, he came along and he picked up a gang of us that came up, and we got into a group, with the guards that were leading him. And we went in the back end of a place that had chicken coops but there were no chickens, they were empty, and they had a lot of the [prisoners from the 106th Division].

It was starting to snow, and the chaplain told the officer who opened the door that he'd like for the men to come inside. The officer said, "Are they enlisted men, or are they officers?"

He said, "They're a mixture of both."

He said, "Well, they're not coming in here." He said according to the Geneva Treaty, enlisted men are supposed to be separated from the officers.

The chaplain said, "I'll tell you what. My name is . . ." And he gave it, I have it in the book. "You can do what you want to me, but on Christmas Eve, the holiest day of the year, you would take and keep these men out in that snow? Baloney," he said. "They're going in."

We went in, and he turned around and he lit candles, and he said,

"We're going to have a nonsectarian service for Christmas Eve." Well, there wasn't a dry eye in that place.

There was an air raid during the service, and the guard came in and said, "You put those candles out or I'll kill you."

He said, "If you have to kill me on this night, kill me. My name," he says, "will still be here, and my soul will be up in heaven. You do what you want."

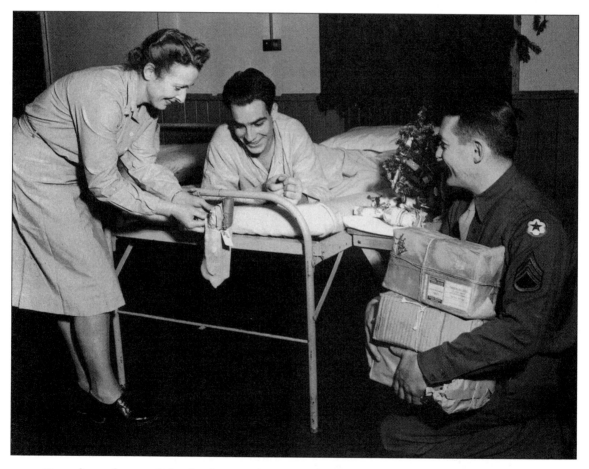

Countless volunteers helped to keep up the spirits of servicemen wounded in action in World War II, and they were especially needed at Christmastime, when holiday spirits conflicted with the harsh reality of pain and the uncertainty about what the future might hold. There were 670,846 wounded Americans in World War II, more than three times as many as in World War I.

★ ★ ★

A Doctor Says Farewell

THE GERMAN COUNTEROFFENSIVE began on December 16, 1944, not long after I arrived in France. The Germans crashed through our lines at the most unexpected place and time. It was in the dead of winter, the weather was horrible, snow was all over the ground, and they just blew through our lines like a dose of salts.

I remember, right before Christmas, being called to the tent of the hospital unit's commanding officer (CO), who told me I would leave the next morning. He explained that the command had come down to all the medical units, requiring them to send every general duty medical officer to a combat unit.

. . . My CO told me that the next morning I would go to an airstrip where I would board a Douglas C-47 transport plane that would take me to Paris, then to my new unit.

That night I had to get my duffel bag packed, but first I went back by the tent where I had patients, many of them Germans, who told me to come back later that night. They had been planning to give me a little something for Christmas, so they went ahead and gave me a program of singing and a plaque one of the German prisoners had carved using a pen knife and a piece of wood taken from a packing case. All these years, I've kept that tiny plaque on my office wall. It shows a woman looking through a window at the shining star of Bethlehem; and in the bottom corner, it says, simply, "Weihnachten 1944." *Weihnachten* means Christmas in German

---

First Lieutenant Charles Schneider, a battalion surgeon with the Eightieth Infantry Division, saw war in all of its horror at the front lines. In December 1944 in the bitter cold of the Ardennes, Schneider treated Allied injured as well as those of the German army. At Christmas he received a surprise.

Christmas Gifts Courtesy of E. B. White

When the essayist and humorist E. B. White looked under the nation's Christmas tree in the winter of 1944, he found special gifts.

THEY ARE NOT WRAPPED AS GIFTS (there was no time to wrap them), but you will find them under the lighted tree with the other presents. They are the extra gifts, the ones with the hard names. Certain towns and villages. Certain docks and installations. Atolls in a sea. Assorted airstrips, beachheads, supply dumps, rail junctions. Here is a gift to hold in your hand—Hill 660. Vital from a strategic standpoint. "From the Marines," the card says. Here is a small strip of the Italian coast. Merry Christmas from the members of the American Fifth (who waded ashore). This is Kwajalein, Maloelap, Wotje. This is Eniwetok . . .

Who wouldn't love the Norman coast for Christmas? Who hasn't hoped for the Atlantic Wall, the impregnable? Here is the whole thing under the lighted tree. First the beaches (greetings from the Navy and the Coast Guard), then the cliffs, the fields behind the cliffs, the inland villages and towns, the key places, the hedgerows, the lanes, the houses, and the barns. Ste. Mère Eglise (with greetings from Omar Bradley and foot soldiers). This Norman cliff (best from the Rangers). St. Jacques de Nehou (from the Eighty-second Airborne Division, with its best) . . .

Still the gifts come. You haven't even noticed the gift of the rivers Marne and Aisne: Château-Thierry, Soissons (this is where you came

The Santa Claus handing out Christmas presents to English children is a member of the 381st Bombardment Group, stationed at Ridgewell, England. The men of the 381st sailed for England aboard the **Queen Elizabeth,** *operating as a troop transport, in May 1943. Within a month they were flying the first of their 296 strategic bombing missions over Germany. Their weapon was the fabled B-17 bomber, nicknamed the "Flying Fortress" because of its substantial armament and excellent record of flying even when hit.*

★ ★ ★

in). Verdun, Sedan (greetings from the American First Army, greetings from the sons of the fathers). Here is a most unusual gift, a bit of German soil. Priceless. A German village, Roetgen . . . there isn't time to look at them all. It will take years. This is a Christmas you will never forget, people have been so generous.

Keith Somerville to Her "Boys" on the Christmas of '44

Keith Somerville once styled herself as a "pencil-packing Mama." Long-time community leader in Bolivar County, Mississippi, well-known daughter of a former United States senator, she gave dedicated support to U.S. troops. She was a Red Cross worker who made surgical dressings; she was a USO hostess at the American Legion; and, in January 1943, she began writing a column called "Dear Boys" for the **Bolivar Commercial.** *Not only did she write the column, she obtained the addresses of servicemen on the front and at U.S. bases and sent the newspapers out herself. "If only one or two boys a week enjoy them, it's well worth my time and effort," she wrote in her journal. After devoting most of her waking moments to the war effort, she stopped long enough during Christmas 1944 to write "God help me to do more . . ."*

January 12, 1945

Dear Boys:

Christmas has come and gone and the new year of 1945 has started. January 1 was a lovely, sunshiny day here, giving promise of good weather, but the radio news from the Western Front did not give us much promise of an early peace. The bowl games on the radio sounded exciting, especially Duke and Alabama in the Sugar Bowl, where they seesawed back and forth (first one ahead, then the other) till Duke finally won out. In New Orleans, where that game was played, they tell me it is the custom to leave Christmas trees up till "Twelfth Night" (January twelfth), which is a custom I wish I'd been reared in, for I always hate to see the Christmas decorations go, especially so this year, for they were a symbol of the happy times my lucky, little Santa-age granddaughters (two, three, and four years old) had with their gifts and their service daddies home for a few days . . .

I come of the school of thought which says it's bad luck to leave the red candles, the holly, and the tree up over the New Year. So on New Year's Eve, as I heard the whistles blow in Times Square (radio) and a lovely voice raised in "The Star-Spangled Banner," I took everything down at my house and carefully packed the few remaining lights and unbroken ornaments away for another year. As I burned the greenery in my fireplace, I tho't of you boys. No, I didn't make any resolutions to break; I just said prayers for your safety and for the peace of this war worn world.

Before closing the books on 1944, I'd like right here to say thanks to each of you who remembered me. I loved your cards, and the knowledge that so many of you, far from home, remembered me gave me a tremendous thrill. I loved those notes some of you wrote on the cards, too, and I am writing each of you personally. A stack of V-mail letters is going out to you today.

Memories of Tin Can Ornaments

Soldiers tried to re-create Christmas any way they could. Tony Valentino, a twenty-year-old marine recovering from wounds suffered overseas, was in Quantico, Virginia, in early 1944 when he met Margery Hunt, a PFC just out of boot camp. Just before shipping out from Washington, D.C., Tony and Margery married and, shortly thereafter, celebrated Christmas.

I spent my nineteenth and twentieth birthdays overseas and came back to the states in late 1943. After recovery in Oak Knoll Hospital and Great Lakes Naval Hospital, I was sent to Quantico, Va.

I was getting ready to ship out again, and Margery wanted to have a Christmas tree. She made ornaments from tin cans from her mess hall.

As a cook at the base, Margery saw more tin cans than Popeye on a good spinach day. The tin got cut into stars, snowflakes, flowers and all the Yuletide patterns. Those ornaments rusted and got lost over the years (though bought ornaments never did shine as brightly), but the memory of the love behind them is always in my heart. Who can say why certain things happen? In my case, I met a special lady while in the Marine Corps [and she made] the Christmas of 1944 our most memorable. ☆

In this ad, the end is near, and hopes are high that it will be joyous when it comes. By Christmas 1944, many Americans were beginning to turn their thoughts to a postwar world. Instead of tanks and planes, consumer goods could once more flow from the factories, with shortages and rationing a thing of the past.

✦ ✦ ✦

Sergeant D. W. Sak of Cincinnati, Ohio, leads Filipinos in Christmas carols at Tacloban City on Leyte, temporary seat of the Commonwealth of the Philippines government.

✦ ✦ ✦

Candlelight Service at Tinian

CBs of the Fiftieth Battalion gather in a makeshift chapel on Tinian in the Marianas Islands to bow their heads in prayer at a candlelight Holy Communion service on Christmas Eve 1944. Never mind that the pews are made of sandbags: The sentiments are real and deeply felt. Tinian, a thirty-nine-square-mile volcanic island 100 miles north of Guam, was captured from the Japanese during 1944. Perhaps nothing better illustrates the strange coexistence of faith and hope with death and destruction that epitomized Christmas on the war front than the activities about to take place on this island. American troops there will be assigned to build the longest runways in the world, from which the **Enola Gay** will take off in August to drop an atomic bomb on Hiroshima.

☆ ☆ ☆

1945

☆ ☆ ☆

Perhaps like no other year in United States history, 1945 brought a whirlwind of events, one following the other like thunderclaps. In early January American soldiers, led by General Douglas MacArthur, invaded Luzon in the Philippines. As he vowed, MacArthur had returned. A month later, President Roosevelt, Prime Minister Churchill, and Soviet leader Joseph Stalin began a wartime conference at Yalta on the Crimea.

The end was near for the Axis powers. On February 14 and 15 Allied planes staged a massive bombing raid on Dresden, Germany. The ensuing firestorm destroyed the German artistic and cultural capital, killing more than 35,000 people.

In early April delegates from some fifty countries began gathering in San Francisco to organize the United Nations. Once again, world leaders struggled to find a way to avert the kind of international nightmare they had just endured. By the summer the U.S. Senate had ratified the United Nations Charter by a vote of 89–2.

On April 12, at Warm Springs, Georgia, Franklin Roosevelt, the thirty-second president of the United States, died of a cerebral hemorrhage at age sixty-three. Upon the president's death, Vice President Harry Truman was sworn in as the nation's thirty-third chief executive. On that same day, the Allied forces liberated Buchenwald and Belsen concentration camps. The photos of the Nazi death camps soon published in newspapers and magazines brought forth to the American people the full horror of the atrocities committed against Jews during the Holocaust.

The banner hanging from General MacArthur's head-quarters in Tokyo is likely to be most appreciated by Allied servicemen and women who have just won the war.

★ ★ ★

As Russian troops approached his Berlin bunker on April 30, master race supremacist Adolf Hitler committed suicide along with his wife of one day, Eva Braun. A week later, on May 7, Germany surrendered unconditionally, ending Hitler's Third Reich.

In a grisly demonstration of what could have been, if the war had reached American soil, a Japanese balloon bomb exploded on Gearhart Mountain in Oregon, killing Elsie Mitchell, the pregnant wife of a minister, and five children who were on a picnic.

On August 6, 1945, the greatest military explosion in world history occurred. A U.S. B-29 Super Fortress called the *Enola Gay* dropped a ten-foot-long atomic bomb, code-named "Little Boy," on Hiroshima, Japan, killing an estimated 140,000 people. It was the first use of a nuclear weapon in warfare, and the blast wiped out four square miles. A second A-bomb was dropped in Nagasaki, Japan, three days later. On August 15, Emperor Hirohito called upon the Japanese people to "bear the unbearable" and lay down their arms. Two weeks later, on September 2, Japan formally surrendered to the United States in ceremonies aboard the USS *Missouri.* At about the same time, Communist guerrilla leader Ho Chi Minh led a successful coup in Vietnam; the French prepared to retaliate.

America was coming home. As soldiers returned, as families struggled to put their lives back into a comfortable routine, as some grieved and others celebrated, all realized the toll taken by war. But they had persevered. And now, for the first time in several years, Fords rolled off the assembly lines.

Art Linkletter starred on the CBS Radio debut of "House Party." The show continued on the air for twenty-two years, including a long stint on CBS Television; also on CBS the "Arthur Godfrey Time" began a twenty-seven-year run. Gimbel Brothers in Philadelphia became the first department store to demonstrate a television set to the public; over a three-week period, more than 25,000 people stopped by to gawk. At the Mississippi-Alabama Dairy Show, a young boy from Memphis, Tennessee, ten-year-old Elvis Presley, made his first public appearance, singing "Old Shep." He won a second-place prize of $5.

And some things never seemed to change. The top-selling song for 1945—Bing Crosby's "White Christmas" again.

"Eternal Father Strong to Save": Lost in the Triangle

The "Devil's Triangle" or the "Bermuda Triangle" is an area in the Atlantic noted for a high incidence of unexplained losses of ships, small boats, and aircraft. The apexes of the triangle are generally accepted to be Bermuda; Miami, Florida; and San Juan, Puerto Rico. The strange disappearances of aircraft and ships within this region have stirred belief in the supernatural qualities of the triangle. Perhaps the most famous of those disappearances was that of "Flight 19," a group of six aircraft filled with servicemen on their way home for Christmas. Bob Woerner, whose friend was lost on that flight, still wonders what happened.

IN DECEMBER 1945 we were all getting ready to go home for Christmas. For most of us in the Combat Aircrewman Training Program at NAS

1943 {

1944 {

1945 {

SICILY!

BURMA!

NORMANDY!

HOLLAND!

Berlin

TOKYO

This 1945 Christmas card is from the WACO Aircraft Company of Troy, Ohio. WACO produced 1,074 of the total 12,000 CG-4 gliders manufactured during WWII. These gliders were just right for bringing a squad of soldiers into action, or for delivering a vehicle or artillery piece too heavy to be dropped by parachute.

✫ ✫ ✫

Banana River, Florida, we hadn't been home since we started the program in September 1944. The war was over, most of the flying had stopped, and in 1946 we would all be getting orders to transition to the separation center nearest our home as "ship's company" until we had enough points to get discharged.

Fred Zywicki and I had trained together since boot camp at Jax in September '44. Then on to Norman, Okla. for AOM "A" School and Radar School. Gunnery School was next at Yellow Water, then on to Banana River after a TDY at NAS Melbourne, Florida. We were in the same crew, CAC 88-I and flew many patrols together during the three months of Operational Training. We were the two ordnance waist gunners and doubled also in the upper deck . . . Fred was looking forward to getting home to the Chicago he had left 16 months before.

On December 5th, I was assigned to the Beaching crew, cursing the PBM-3s that still didn't have wheels. Other members of the crew were assigned to other "non-flying" duties. But some stayed on standby, including Fred—I was lucky.

Somewhat to the south, on that day, at NAS Ft. Lauderdale, five TBM Avenger Torpedo Bombers were warming up to take their last training hop. The Navy and Marine Combat Aircrewman needed one more flight to qualify for their wings. And the pilots, except for the flight leader, needed one more navigational training flight to finish. One marine missed the flight. This was the famous "Flight 19," a composite training flight of both Navy and Marine Corps airmen, that would become the subject of every "Devil's Triangle" story on TV and books for decades to come. After flying eastward and then northward for some hours, they became lost. They reported trouble with their compasses and couldn't orient directions correctly. As nightfall approached they were almost out of gas—and then all Florida east coast bases lost radio contact with them.

At NAS Banana River, Florida, two PBMs were alerted to take off on a Search and Rescue operation down to North of the Bahamas to fly a "box" pattern. Their long range meant that they could fly all night if necessary. They were fully gassed. They passed all pre-flight checks. The crew on PBM No. 59225 was made up of our crew and other volunteers. Curiously, there were five pilots, and eight crewmen. We seldom flew with thirteen, and never with five pilots.

Both PBMs took off and headed off in different directions. Radar had them both plotted— Suddenly, PBM 59225 disappeared from the radar. A merchant ship, the SS *Gaines Mills,* reported seeing a massive explosion high in the sky, which then gravitated down to the ocean and continued to burn with flames one hundred feet high.

A large search and rescue mission was already being formed by sea for the five TBMs. In the morning, the USS *Solomons* CVE-67 approached the approximate site of the crash and found only a small oil slick, no debris, no survivors. The plane and crew had apparently vaporized— The other PBM and the search vessels and aircraft continued their search for the TBMs for several days with no results.

On this day, December 5, 1945, six aircraft and twenty-seven men disappeared and the cause has never been established. They joined the many other aircrewmen who also disappeared in flight in this area known as "The Devil's Triangle," some were other PBMs from Banana River. The Navy convened a Board of Inquiry, which is available on Microfiche, but little was found to add to the facts.

Alfred Zywicki, S1/c (AOM)(CA), USNR, would not be going home for Christmas.

Riding the Rails Home

By the time of the Second World War, the siren's call of the railroad had gripped Americans for many generations. The railroad's steel arms reached nearly every county in the United States, bringing not only mobility but an almost mystical fascination with its power and speed. Bob

★ 1945 ★

Williams, a soldier stationed in the Philippines, stepped onto a train in California for his ride home to the Midwest after the war. He still salutes it as he would a friend—train "Number Two."

In August 1945, when World War II ended, I was six thousand miles from home on the island of Luzon in the Philippines. I had been in the Philippines since the Leyte invasion the previous October, and I was ready to return to my family.

Three months later, in November, I made a mental note—a vow I shared with no one—that if I could get away from Luzon by Thanksgiving, I would be home for Christmas. I couldn't do it alone. It would take a lot of help from many sources. But that was my hope and my dream.

The USS *General Howze* got away from San Fernando on the Lingayan Gulf early in Thanksgiving week. This is a start. The troopship arrived at San Pedro, California, around December 14. Getting close, but still time. After a short stay at Camp Anza, a thousand or more of us loaded on a troop train and headed east on the Santa Fe, bound for discharge and homes across the land.

All kinds of rolling stock had been pressed into service to "get the boys home for Christmas," and I was assigned to a Central Railroad of New Jersey commuter coach—straight-back seats, with armrest dividers between them. That was to be my means of travel for the 1800 miles or so to St. Louis. I didn't mind—I would have ridden a Norfolk Western hopper car, I think, just to be able to get home for that special holiday. My destination: Decatur, Illinois.

To escape the discomfort of the crowded coach, one of my companions and I volunteered for KP. Both of us were staff sergeants and had not served in that capacity for months. Nonetheless, it seemed better than sitting in the restrictive confines of an uncomfortable chair, so we went to one of the kitchen cars at the head of the train. I recall sitting in the open door of the car peeling potatoes with the cold air rushing in as the train climbed Cajon Pass. I had been over the pass on the California Limited in the summer of 1941, but I had been in a reclining-seat, air-conditioned coach. This was natural air-conditioning.

In Kansas City the train was split. Some of it went on to Chicago on the Santa Fe, the troops bound for Fort Sheridan north of the city. The rest of us would go to Jefferson Barracks south of St. Louis to be discharged. Our section sat in the dark for what seemed to be hours someplace in the Kansas City yards of the Missouri Pacific before we finally headed east. An overnight run to St. Louis, a quick dash to Jefferson Barracks, and we were on our last leg of a trip home. Still time to make it for Christmas.

There was a lot of paperwork associated with getting out of the Army: "Sign up for the reserves?" No. "Keep your GI insurance?" Yes—it was still cheap at the price. "Taking any weapons or souvenirs with you?" No. "What size clothing do you wear?" Did it make any difference? You got what was next on the pile in the supply room anyway.

It was December 24. Time was running out. The afternoon raced on as we waited for our issue of clothes, copies of papers, a photocopy of

It's a barracks, not the warmth of the family living room back home. And that's a cinder-block backdrop, not the coziness of the familiar four walls that encompassed the world in which they grew up. But these WACs are making the most of it. They've got a tree, some presents, and each other's company in this wartime Yuletide season.

★ ★ ★

Holiday Greetings

AND WITH THEM OUR THANKS

With best wishes for a happy holiday season, we extend to everyone our sincere appreciation for your cooperation during the difficult war years.

Your patience lessened the tremendous job which confronted us. Now, with the return of peace, we will devote all our efforts and nation-wide facilities to the sole purpose of providing a fine transportation service.

RAILWAY EXPRESS AGENCY

NATION-WIDE · RAIL-AIR SERVICE

our discharge, and a host of other things that had to be done to clear us of our military obligations. Finally, just before 5 P.M., the last bit of business was completed and we were civilians again. We were given vouchers to exchange for train tickets and herded out in a loose formation to a platform where a line of buses waited, all bound for the massive St. Louis Union Station.

I had been through Union Station four times during the war. I had ridden MoPac's Sunshine Special to my post in Texas after two furloughs during the time when people were supposed to ask themselves "Is this trip necessary?" but this would be my most important visit.

There was now no question—I would be home for Christmas! My vow was fulfilled! The question now was, can I make it

The Railway Express Agency was the product of war—World War I—when the government in 1918 consolidated various railway express services to achieve greater efficiency in the shipment of material by what was then the country's most important means of interstate transport. GIs who fought in World War II and had been to college might have seen the company's ads in their 1930s college newspapers, suggesting that students could take care of their laundry by shipping it home to mom and having her send it back via Railway Express. This ad at Christmas 1945 is yet another sign that things will be getting back to normal, when the railroads will be less a vital cog in the national defense, giving priority to the shipment of war matériel, and more the means by which people separated from loved ones can play Santa Claus with the prompt delivery of Christmas gifts.

★ ★ ★

home in time for Christmas Eve? My family always exchanged gifts then, with Christmas day reserved for eating. I would eat. And eat and eat. But whether I would get home for the gift exchange depended on one thing—an old friend of mine, Wabash No. 2. Technically the Detroit Limited, "Big Two" was the overnight St. Louis–Detroit train. The Wabash Railroad dominated Decatur, with four routes, its major locomotive shops, and a huge freight yard, and I had known Number Two since I was old enough to hear and recognize a train's whistle. My pop introduced me to it.

Big Two was due out of St. Louis Union Station at about 6:15 P.M., and our bus had a long trip from South St. Louis to downtown. Gasoline was more readily available than it had been during the war years, and the streets were jammed with automobiles.

Union Station was also crowded, as it had been all through the war years. Sixteen trunkline railroads scheduled about 160 trains a day into and out of it. I pushed and shoved my way through the crowd at the door and entered the massive structure. My sweep-second-hand watch, with its plastic crystal cracked and scratched from too much insect repellent rubbed on it over the previous eighteen months, was still readable. The time was almost 6:25 P.M.—too late to catch Big Two. Nonetheless, I hurried to the nearest ticket window and waited until I stood before the agent to exchange my voucher for a ticket.

"What time does the Wabash Midnight leave for Chicago?" I asked. That was my best hope now. I knew I could get to Decatur, about 115 miles up the line, sometime around 3 o'clock Christmas morning.

The agent thought a few seconds, took a quick look at my voucher, and said, "You're going to Decatur, aren't you?"

"Yes," I replied.

"The Detroit train hasn't left yet. If you hurry you might still be able to get on it! Get your ticket from the conductor." He did not call it "the Detroit Limited" or "number two." It was "the Detroit train." But I knew what it was.

I turned from the counter without even thanking him. I dragged my canvas duffel bag with my name and serial number freshly stenciled on it across the concourse and headed for the gate from which No. 2 would leave. I threaded my way through waiting passengers, and as I approached the gate, I could see the drumhead on the back of the last Pullman with the Wabash flag and the words "Detroit Limited." My old friend was still there!

★ 1945 ★

All roads' passenger trains backed into Union Station. This took a little longer if you were in a hurry to get off, but outbound trains could head right out and be on their way with a minimum of wasted time. This also eliminated the need for passengers to walk by the hissing, steaming locomotive as they made their way along the platform.

I dashed toward the head of the train, where I knew the Decatur passengers would be loaded—I had seen travelers get off dozens of times at the Wabash depot in Decatur.

Why the train was delayed I will never know. It may have been waiting for a connection from the southwest, or for a Kansas City train to come in with passengers bound for Fort Wayne or Detroit. It might have been waiting for me! After all, we were old friends. Whatever the reason, I spotted an empty seat, heaved my duffel bag up in the luggage rack over it, and sat down, heaving a big sigh of relief that I was aboard and headed home for Christmas Eve.

We paused at Delmar Station, then crossed the Mississippi River to Granite City, Illinois, and sped on up the line to Litchfield and Taylorville. I busied myself with pinning my two rows of campaign ribbons on the oversized olive drab "blouse" I had been issued. I had hoped for a more modern Eisenhower jacket, but the Quartermaster Corps at Jefferson Barracks was out. The blouse had someone else's name marked on it with permanent ink. He had probably turned it in for an Eisenhower jacket earlier, but I didn't care. This would be the only time I would wear my uniform with its ribbons and battle stars on it in public. The "ruptured duck" emblem—a gold eagle woven on a diamond-shaped patch—was sewed over the right pocket, indicating I had been discharged. But in that coach that night, no one even saw it. Their thoughts, in most cases, like mine, were on getting home for Christmas.

Number Two rounded the curve into Decatur, thundering across the Sangamon River bridge. It whistled for Wood Street, William Street, and North Street, cruising past the Millikin University campus. It slowed as it reached Mercer Street tower, where the St. Louis and Kansas City lines joined, then headed east toward the depot.

Even in the darkness, I could distinguish familiar landmarks: Decatur Milling Company; North Main Street and the view south into the business district; Water Street and the Avon and Empress theater marquees, now dark; the Railway Express building; and finally the Wabash depot.

I stood, trembling slightly. I retrieved my duffel bag, then waited with some impatience for other passengers to get off. I bent and tried to see if anyone was waiting on the platform, but the reflection on the windows from the lights inside made it impossible to see. I had called during the day and had left word I might be on No. 2, so I presumed someone would be there.

Finally, down the steps, onto the steel stepbox, and down on the platform. I was home. And I was met. The folks had checked with the Wabash and learned the train was running late, so they thought I might have made it. Reunion. Love shared. Joy. Tears.

We didn't wait to see Big Two leave—there were too many things to catch up on. But before we left, I turned and saluted my old friend. It would be my last salute while still in uniform, and it could not have been presented to a more deserving recipient.

Number Two would soon head out and disappear into the darkness of East Decatur yard. It had 375 miles to go, and its marker lights would fade this night as it bore other passengers to happy reunions like the one it had made possible for me. Those marker lights would never fade from my memory, though. Nor would all the happy memories I carry for this old friend my Pop introduced me to when I was a kid lying in bed listening to its whistle as it thundered into town.

A Small Voice; A Big Homecoming

Many servicemen returned home after the war to see their children for the first time. Joyce Edwardson of New London, Minnesota, remembers the phone call in which her husband first heard the voice of his daughter.

IT WAS CHRISTMAS 1945, World War II was over, but thousands of troops remained in military camps all over America, my husband among them. Our baby daughter was two-months old. Only other families separated involuntarily by the Armed Services know what it is like to face Christmas without each other.

In his latest letter, my husband wrote he would phone me and to have the baby there so he could hear her voice.

When the phone rang, I dutifully held the baby in one arm and the receiver in the other and talked into the wall phone. She remained quiet, waving her arms and wriggling but no sounds. My husband and I spoke of our loneliness, the activities in his camp and the Christmas dinner menus, both there and with our families. Still, baby was quiet.

"Can't you make her talk?" he inquired.

"No," I said. "She's happy right where she is."

Just then, having had enough of being on my shoulder in one position, she let out a wail into his waiting ear. His chuckle told me of his joy.

With baby's crying, our conversation was over and we said goodbye. We were still lonely but we knew the next Christmas would be much better for us and for our child in a world that was full of hope.

Lonely in the Philippines

Ensign Charles Newberry had spent the previous two Christmas seasons away from his California home. Although the war was over now, he would not be home for Christmas again. In a Quonset hut on Leyte Gulf, the Philippines, he sat down in late November 1945 and wrote his thoughts about Christmas and home.

ONE SHORT MONTH AWAY and some six thousand miles away from here and it will be Christmas in Southern California! Rain splashing on the windshield, the soft swish of tires on wet pavement, the red and green and yellow and blue lights of the Christmas tree sale lots shining through the rain and dancing on the gutter puddles and the sidewalks. The growing trees on lawns hung with strings of lights which along with the window views of indoor ornamented trees make every street and avenue a Christmas Tree Lane . . .

The downtown shopping crowds on Broadway and Hollywood Boulevard, jamming buses and streetcars and shops. The warm sultry smell in the crowded stores as one comes in from the wintry rainy streets. The misty halos around the street decorations and the neon signs. Jam-packed streets, automobiles crawling along, honking, and the trolley bells, and the tinkling of the [Salvation] Army tambourines. Packages of colored paper, tinsel and the thousand-colored ribbons.

And small children and Santa Clauses and the toy department and school programs for Christmas . . .

The "Merry Christmas" and the "Happy New Year" in speech and in print—the carols and the stories and the signs. Christmas cheer and the drunks. Blazing fires of papier-mache logs and red light bulbs and cellophane and the warm fires in homes, red and yellow and green, when the sap comes out. Flames and the shadows flickering across the

Christmas dinner is served up en masse to hospital personnel in the mess hall of Camp McQuaide, California. This installation on Monterey Bay near Watsonville, named for a chaplain, was opened in 1938. The hospital was set on a height, overlooking the Pacific, with the foothills of the Santa Cruz Mountains as a backdrop. But it was hardly an idyllic sight during the early 1940s. Once the United States entered the war, the camp was crammed with soldiers in training for combat. Then, in 1943, a large detention center for army deserters was constructed on the grounds. Camp McQuaide was closed in 1946.

★ ★ ★

room. And candlelight and incense and presents under the tree. And poinsettias . . .

The chill in the air. The feeling of a real holiday spirit—more rain—and snow in the mountains and last-minute cards . . . And visits, friends, relatives and the people next door—the candy and nuts and the big dinner and taking it easy, just relaxing. Eggnogs and wine and rum and that rosy feeling. Christmas at home . . .

Christmas in the Philippines—drink, reminiscent thoughts, a day off, a good dinner, perhaps a card game, carols on the radio, more drinks and to bed, for tomorrow we build. Am I ever getting sentimental! Or maybe homesick is the word—or maybe I'm just fed up with being out here or something.

Christmas in Tokyo

Following the attack on Pearl Harbor, the Japanese launched an assault on the Philippines. General Douglas MacArthur's 12,000 American and 35,000 Filipino troops put up fierce resistance, beating back a vastly superior Japanese invasion force and delaying the Japanese timetable of conquest. In February 1942, under instructions from General Eisenhower, MacArthur, his wife and son, and members of his staff left the Philippines, which soon fell to the Japanese. However, MacArthur pledged, "I shall return," and he kept that promise.

On October 20, 1944, he landed with his forces on Leyte, one of the Philippine islands. Less than a year later, on September 2, 1945, as commander in chief in the Pacific, MacArthur accepted Japan's surrender. Mervyn Horder, a Royal Air Force Wing Commander under Lord Mountbatten, remembers a British tea party and Christmas celebration in Tokyo after the war. One of the guests was General MacArthur.

WHEN ALL HAD ARRIVED, we proceeded to tea—a British tea provided by Japanese staff out of who-knows-what ceremonial recipe books, even down to the white-iced Christmas fruitcake. Grown-ups waited on the children, and though there was little of what could be called an exchange of diplomatic ideas among our guests, there was certainly none at all of that preoccupied silence which is the usual mark of high-level gastronomic appreciation. The noise was incessant; most troublesome of all was a little blue-eyed Norwegian devil who resorted repeatedly to that idle drumming on the table with a teaspoon so beloved of the attention-seeking young. We pacified him as adults have pacified obstreperous children throughout the ages, by removing the offending instrument by force and filling his mouth with cake; but he liked cake, and resumed the drumming with another spoon as often as he could.

After tea we had a conjurer—a little old man who kept insisting in his three or four words of sibilant English that he was Chinese, not Japanese. Whichever it was, he was at the head of his profession. Less than five feet high, he was muffled from head to foot in a quilted gown, and the climax of his act (which began with the usual paper, silk and coin tricks) was to produce from the folds of this gown no less than five outsize enamel wash-basins. There was no doubt of the reality of these basins, each of which he tapped with his fist and passed to us nonchalantly for inspection before stacking them on a convenient chair. They were perfectly ordinary enamel basins, as prosaic and uncollapsible as such things always are, the biggest about eighteen inches across. He produced them all in dead silence, with an expressionless face; then followed them, also from the folds of his gown, with four white pigeons which, after fluttering round to show they were real too, sat on his shoulders and pecked him amiably on his cheeks. Thus escorted he made his triumphant exit.

We then turned to what we luckily found to be one of the few truly international and universally understood occupations for the young—musical chairs. For music we had available, it is true, the fondest treasure of the British Embassy in Tokyo, a scratchy old record of "God Save the King" chanted in English by a patriotic gathering of eighty Japanese schoolchildren about 1928 . . . but since this might have been construed as propaganda, and could not in any case be described as music—it was indeed one of the most horrible sounds I have ever heard—we fell back on another record dredged up from somewhere, one of the more innocent offerings of the old Savoy Orpheans.

In his 1945 Christmas message, General MacArthur acknowledges the obvious gift for which all are giving thanks on this holiday: The war has come to a victorious end for the Allies. But the wish that had not yet been fulfilled for many was a place on one of the countless ships now ferrying men across the Pacific and Atlantic to that last trip home. It would be 1946 before many would enjoy that pleasure.

✫ ✫ ✫

☆ ☆ ☆

Arthur MacArthur, son of General Douglas MacArthur, celebrates Christmas in occupied Japan. Arthur, named for the General's father, also a prominent figure in the American military, is already making use of one of his gifts, a typewriter, which only months earlier might have been unavailable even to MacArthur's son because of rationing. The same holds true for that shiny new bicycle next to the Christmas tree.

As I stood operating the portable gramophone—needle down, music; needle up, no music—I could not help drawing a sombre parallel between the antics of the children and the exactly similar manoeuvres of displacement and counter-displacement on which their parents were daily engaged in the chancelleries of the world. Sombre parallel or no sombre parallel, however, nothing inhibited the will to win of a portly young lady from one of the South American republics whose natural breadth of beam gave her an unfair advantage where chairs were concerned; and nothing inhibited the piercing cries and squawks in every known language which rent the air, and drove the General [MacArthur] temporarily into exile in another room.

This was the scene of deafening international confusion which was suddenly interrupted by two loud and imperious knocks, evidently on one of the windows giving onto the garden outside. This was my cue to dart forward, throw back the curtains and reveal, dimly outlined against the dark and the snow, the figure of—who could it be— Yes, Santa Claus himself. We had spent hours gluing dabs of cotton wool on the panes of the relevant window just in case, but in the event nature herself took over and favoured us with a downpour of huge, lazy, swirling flakes that Drury Lane could not have bettered. With elaborate gestures for the children's benefit I signalled to Santa to come round to the front door, which he did—stepping into a jeep on the way. We had given up our first idea of providing him with dog transport, after considering the unwholesome collection of curs which was all that bomb-ravaged Tokyo seemed likely to be able to assemble. Our Santa would be modern, bringing modern gifts, in a modern vehicle, to modern children.

The front door of our house was of frosted glass, and the vermilionclad figure (in fact it was the Chief of Staff of our Mission and no more superbly red-nosed, ingratiating and benevolent Santa Claus can ever have existed) was soon seen again arriving in his jeep, stepping out with one of the Embassy mailbags across his shoulder and demanding admittance. From then on the children took charge. They opened the door, they thronged round their visitor so that he could hardly move and did their best to prevent him ever getting to his pre-arranged position on the main stairway from which he was to dole out his presents.

By an odd coincidence his sack contained exactly the same number of presents as there were children. Our chief difficulty had been with the ten-year-old son of General MacArthur himself; he was an only boy, the apple of his father's eye, and it was rumoured that the General habitually gave him a present of some kind every day of the week as he left the house to go to work. What then could we poor British drum up to satisfy so well-endowed a youth? Our answer was luckily the right one—a bow and arrow, flown up specially from Shanghai in the luggage of a new cipher girl. From the boy's incredulous and delighted amazement it was clear that his father had not yet thought of that one.

Santa's verbal communications during this time had been confined to friendly gurgles, grunts and booms in what must be supposed to be one of the Arctic vernaculars; but when his distribution of gifts was over, he permitted himself a highly moral little speech in English to the effect that he could not stay since there were many other children, including Japanese children, on his visiting list, and he would have to nip off to fill his sack again.

It was certainly part of the success of the operation that he was not in the house more than five minutes—no time for his clothes (hired from the American PX) to be pulled to pieces revealing the British colonel's uniform underneath, no time to answer awkward questions or accept impossible commissions, no time for his magic to evaporate. The jeep began to blow its horn insistently outside. Santa picked his way downstairs through his admirers, opened the door, blew kisses all round, stepped into his vehicle and was lost to sight down the drive.

In no time at all—just as well, since we had no further attractions to offer—hats, coats and mufflers were being fetched, parents being summoned on the none too efficient Tokyo telephone exchange and the house emptied, leaving the hosts to recover with a dram or two among the streamers, trampled paper hats and torn cracker-ends.

At supper I thought I might profitably tease the General a bit: "You remember saying you hated Christmas, sir?"

"Not at all. This is the kind of Christmas I like."

Bob Hope Entertains the Troops

Bob Hope, seen entertaining the troops in the rain, is said to be the most honored figure in the history of show business. The British-born comedian, star of vaudeville, radio, and films by the time he was known as "GI Bob" in World War II, gave his first camp show for soldiers at March Field in California in 1941. The government asked that he remain a civilian in World War II, working to promote the sale of war bonds and to entertain the troops. Bob Hope is said to have performed for American servicemen in World War II under every imaginable condition, even telling jokes while standing on the wing of a seaplane. On one trip across the Pacific, he traveled 30,000 miles, playing 100 shows in fifty-one days.

★ ★ ☆

General Patton
Laid to Rest

George S. Patton was welcomed to the United States as a hero following the war. But back in Germany, he had expressed the view that the United States and Britain should consider rearming the Germans to fight off the Russian threat. His remarks cost him the command of his beloved Third Army; official Washington didn't quite know what to do with the brilliant but outspoken general in peacetime. Although throughout Patton's military career he had exposed himself to danger repeatedly, it was a traffic accident, not the war, that took his life. In December 1945, a year after his Christmas rescue of Bastogne had begun, his car was hit by a truck and he was severely injured. He died from the injuries on December 21 and was buried in Luxembourg, a country that considers him their liberator. At the funeral that day was a reporter from the **Washington Times-Herald** *who filed the story on Christmas Eve. The reporter was Walter Cronkite.*

GEN. GEORGE S. PATTON joined the dead heroes of his 3d army today beneath the thick, red clay of the Ardennes, where they had fought together just a year ago.

Patton was buried the morning of this Christmas Eve in what he himself once had called "damned poor tank country and damned bad weather." But he was buried in a precision-like military ceremony, touched by pomp and tendered by grief.

Big generals and little soldiers were there, as were the royalty and the commoners of this tiny country from which Patton drove the Germans in that crucial battle last Christmastide.

But the focal figure, standing there under the dark sky against the background of green hills, was Patton's widow. A raw wind, whirling across the top of the blue on which the cemetery is located, ruffled Mrs. Patton's veil as she watched the ceremony at the grave, no different from the 7,933 others topped by white crosses.

Her eyes were red, but for the rest she was the same good soldier her husband had been.

In the final minute of the ceremony M/Sgt. William G. Meeks, the negro from Junction City, Kansas, who had served Patton faithfully as his orderly for eight years, presented the general's widow with the flag that had draped the coffin.

There were tears in Meeks' eyes. His face was screwed up with strain. He bowed slowly, and handed the flag to Mrs. Patton. Then he saluted stiffly to her. For an instant their eyes met and held.

Meeks turned away, a twelve-man firing squad raised its rifles and a three-round volley of salutes echoed into the Luxembourg hills.

The bugler played the soft, sad notes of "taps."

The twenty-five-minute burial ceremony was over. It was 10:15 A.M. in Luxembourg (4:15 A.M. EST).

The train bearing Patton's body arrived in the city of Luxembourg early this morning, and the procession from the station to the cemetery, ten miles east of Hamm, began at 9:15.

There were sixty-eight military vehicles and twenty-two limousines

★ ★ ★
The coffin of General George Patton, which was borne by train on Christmas Eve to the Luxemborg cemetary where many of his men were buried.

in the cortege, which passed slowly before crowds of citizens of the duchy. Patton's body was atop a half-track, as it was when it was borne through the streets of Heidelberg yesterday. The men of Luxembourg doffed their hats as it passed. Some, still in Allied uniforms, saluted him, soldier to soldier.

The cortege went through the center of the picturesque capital, passing at one point within two blocks of the headquarters where Patton directed his counteroffensive during the battle of the bulge. At another time, the procession passed along the former Adolf Hitler Strasse, now known as Avenue de Liberté.

It rained steadily this morning until just before the funeral party left the station. Then the rain stopped, but the skies remained leaden and forbidding. The air was damp and cold.

The shops of Luxembourg were closed, and black crepe hung from private homes and official buildings. All the flags in the city were at half-staff.

One Luxembourg woman, Miss Jane Wagener, a gray-haired lady of fifty years or so, was at the cemetery before dawn, just as the last preparations for the funeral were being completed. Two hours she waited in the driving rain and longer than that in the bitter cold to pay her respects to Patton.

"We consider him our liberator," she explained.

As the funeral procession left Luxembourg city and drove along a narrow road into the Ardennes hills, a battery of French 105 artillery somewhere in the distance roared a final seventeen-gun salute.

The last salvo had just echoed through the pines when the cortege turned through the cemetery gate and up the grave-lined road . . .

Mrs. Patton took a last look at the casket while an aide placed a wreath of camelias *[sic]* on the top. The coffin was not lowered into the grave because of the wet weather. The general's widow returned to her limousine where, for ten minutes, she received the condolences of the visiting generals.

Then she drove to the Luxembourg station to entrain for Paris. From there, reports said tonight, she took a plane from Orly Airfield for the United States. That was Mrs. Patton's Christmas Eve.

Among the Pattons, this isn't the best of Christmases for either man or beast. A month after the automobile accident that killed General Patton, his dog, Willie, lies besides his master's personal belongings, awaiting shipment home. Patton had owned several bull terriers over the years, including one named Tank that he had bought for his daughter. The General bought Willie on March 4, 1944, naming him for William the Conqueror. Willie's somewhat pugnacious appearance fitted in well with his owner's demeanor. The dog wore jingle bells on his collar and is said to have possessed his own set of dog tags.

★ ★ ★

The President to His Daughter

It seemed like an eternity since that Christmas Eve four years earlier when President Roosevelt and Prime Minister Winston Churchill, in the wake of the Pearl Harbor attack, had participated in the White House Christmas tree–lighting ceremony. On December 23, 1945, President Harry Truman prepared to address the country at the first Christmas celebration since the U.S. entry into the war; after a brisk walk on the icy paths behind the White House to survey the Christmas tree, he sat down to write a letter to his daughter, Margaret.

Dear Margie:

You'll never know how much your dad appreciated that nice letter, written on the train. It must have been rough over the mountains. I have been in that rear car when the booster engine went to work. It really does shake you up. Sometimes they put it ahead of the diesel, but I imagine the train was too long and they were afraid of pulling the diesel too. So you had a good shaking up. Mr. Clark told me that he saw you on the train. He is one of my cabinet [members] who is for the President and what he is trying to do . . .

I just now went out and took a walk. It is cold as mischief. I looked over the Christmas tree, and walked around the back yard— four Secret Service men and two policemen came along—to keep me from slipping on the ice I guess. A crowd did collect at the back fence. So I guess they were right.

The stage is set up south of the fountain, and one of the pine trees down by the fence is all decorated, and I have to light it and make a speech to the nation tomorrow at 5:16 P.M.

Hope to see you the next day. Kiss Mamma and tell all your aunts & uncles hello, and call up your country grandma and say hello to your city one.

Lots of love, Dad

These German prisoners are packing Christmas candy for French children, donated by GIs. In a part of the war that is not widely known, about 400,000 German prisoners, mostly from the North Africa and Normandy campaigns, were shipped to the United States and put to work on farms, in lumber mills, and at other jobs from 1943 to 1945, often filling in for American boys who had been sent overseas to fight against the Axis powers. The prisoners were paid $.80 a day in scrip, redeemable at their prison camp canteens. In an unsuccessful program, the U.S. government sought to indoctrinate them in the virtues of American democracy (technically a violation of the Geneva Convention). ✳ ✳ ✳

Alive: Wounded Vets Celebrate Christmas

The statistics seem almost incomprehensible. World War II, fought by fifty-seven Allied and Axis countries, had claimed 15 million military personnel killed and missing and an estimated twice that number of

*civilian deaths from bombings, starvation, and murder. A reporter from the **Washington Times-Herald** walked through Walter Reed Hospital on Christmas Eve 1945 talking with some of the survivors.*

WHILE THOUSANDS WORSHIP at Christmas services in Washington churches today, giving thanks for peace and the safe return of loved ones from world battlefields, a host of men, most of them maimed by war's tools of destruction, lie bedridden in Walter Reed Hospital.

It would not seem strange to most people if these men were despondent. No one could blame them if they were jealous—even resentful—of the joy throughout the land on the first peaceful Christmas in five years.

But they aren't downhearted at all. And that seems strange until one talks to them.

Then, as they relate how they spent last Christmas, their happiness is very clear and understandable.

They are alive, and they are home in their native land, and they are going to get well again.

Remember Christmas, 1944 . . . ?

Bill O'Connell is twenty. He has laughing eyes, black hair, and a flashing smile. A girl would call him "handsome." Men would appraise him as a clean, husky, and intelligent kid.

Last Christmas Bill lay paralyzed and unconscious in a hospital in France. The medics wouldn't have given a plugged nickel for his chances to live.

Bill was an infantryman with the fifth Ranger Battalion, attached to Patton's 3d army. Near Saarbrücken, a German machine-gun bullet ploughed through his head from the right side to the left. Four other slugs ripped through a leg, shattering the bones. According to the rule books, he should have been dead.

That was the spot Bill was in last Christmas.

Surgeons at White Sulphur Springs General Hospital put the finishing touches on a miraculous job last August and Bill came home to visit his parents, Capt. and Mrs. William O'Connell, and his sister, Yolanda, ten, at their home, 1823 North Fifteenth St., Arlington. Captain O'Connell is stationed at the Army War College here.

Bill fell while he was home and broke the fragile bones that the surgeons had mended. That's why he's in Walter Reed today.

"But," he said with a grin yesterday, "it'll be O.K. I'm a lucky guy to be here at all. Tomorrow's Christmas, and mom and dad and the kid sister will be over. What's wrong with that setup?"

As Bill finished his story, General Eisenhower, chief of staff, U.S. Army, strode into the ward, unannounced and unexpected. "Ike" had come to visit "his boys" on Christmas Eve.

The No. 1 man in the greatest army in the world didn't miss a man. At every bedside in the hospital Ike stopped to shake a hand, chat a little and give each patient a heartening "Merry Christmas."

"It's certainly a better Christmas this year for all of us," he said, and hustled off on his round of bedside visits.

Today is the first Christmas in the U.S. in three years for Pfc. Cecil E. Massey, 30, of Norfolk, Virginia. He's in a bed and one leg, cruelly ripped by Japanese bullets, is suspended in a network of pulleys, ropes and braces from a wooden framework overhead.

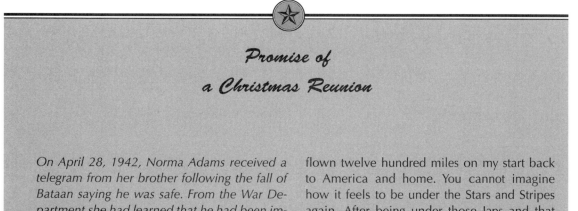

Promise of a Christmas Reunion

On April 28, 1942, Norma Adams received a telegram from her brother following the fall of Bataan saying he was safe. From the War Department she had learned that he had been imprisoned by the Japanese. Well after the formal surrender of the Japanese in 1945, Norma Adams had not heard from her brother again. In October the letter came.

Dear Sister,

Just to let you know I am well and am the happiest man in the world. I hope this finds you and the family well and happy. I have just flown twelve hundred miles on my start back to America and home. You cannot imagine how it feels to be under the Stars and Stripes again. After being under those Japs and that ball of fire they call the Rising Sun for more than three years. At present I am resting in an Army hospital. There is nothing seriously wrong with me—just tired. As soon as the weather clears up I will fly to Manila in the Philippines. I hope to be home by Christmas. If I am we will have a real one. So let the people back there know I am coming back. ★

He was grinning from ear to ear, so help me. Why?

Massey was shot in the same thigh on Saipan and again on Okinawa, serving with the 27th infantry division. Since the last wound cut him down, abscesses have prevented a bone-grafting operation.

"Now," he said cheerfully, "the medics think the infection has cleared up and they can go ahead. That'll be the best Christmas present I ever expect to get."

Toward Tolerance: Looking to the Children

What were Americans to make of this enormous sacrifice? What lessons, especially for parents, should they take away from these traumatic years? In the Christmas issue of **Parents Magazine**, *the editorial page offered an insightful essay authored by "A Mother." The piece was introduced with a quote from a Massachusetts preacher and the author of the lyrics to "O Little Town of Bethlehem," Philip Brooks: "The future of the race marches forward on the feet of little children."*

JOY TO ALL PEOPLE
By a Mother

The festival of the eternal and immortal Child is with us again, for long ago in Bethlehem a Child was born who is still the promise of great joy to all people. And parents the world over look with yearning hope to children who will remake the world.

But the children can't do it alone. Not when they are daily witnesses to the blindness and ignorance of elders. It is this sort of thing that does the damage: "The little house down the street is being built by a Greek. All Greeks are dishwashers." "I'm not going to take your suit to that tailor. You can't trust a Jew." "That part of town is dreadful. Negroes live there so I don't suppose you can expect anything else."

Small talk, this is, but significant. The small talk of well-dressed young mothers driving the children home from school; of successful businessmen, fathers out for a walk with their sons; of fond grandmothers doing a few errands with a youngster or two in tow.

All this is so tragically familiar that we can't dismiss it calmly as happening somewhere else. These scraps of conversation were overheard in a city where schools, social agencies and churches have worked together to build a program for clear thinking and understanding attitudes among school children of various nationalities and backgrounds. They're doing a good job as far as they go. Yet at a board meeting of a social agency in that city, a member told a story of her neighbor's young son who brought home a little Negro classmate to lunch.

"We were so amused," the narrator concluded, "because his mother didn't know how to explain to her son that he couldn't do things like that—that you learn one thing at school but do something else at home."

The anecdote needs no comment, but the laughter of the board members is so shocking in its implication that it sounded ugly to those desirous of making theirs a decent community.

"Peace on earth and good will to men" is the beloved theme of the Christmas season, but it would be unintelligent to shut our eyes to the truth that a great body of fear and hate is rising like a tidal wave all over America. War creates insecurity in many ways, and the feeling of insecurity turns swiftly for expression to avenues of mistrust. The housewife, for instance, who is tired and sick of shortages finds it easy to transfer her anger to the market owner who happens to be Jewish. The employer, harassed by restrictions, vents his feelings on the Negro employee whom he hired reluctantly and as a sop to those who believe in fair practice. Disrupted homes, a disturbed and unfamiliar economy, all increase the tendency to blame someone else.

Fear and hate do not have to manifest themselves violently. They are seen in a tone of voice, a gesture of the hand, an expression of the face. Deeper yet, they appear as an attitude of mind that is more contagious than measles or mumps. These so-receptive children of ours—what can we hope for them if, despite the teachings of school and church that all men worship one God, that all have good gifts to share, that all seek happiness and freedom, they still hear at home, where influences are strongest, something that is quite different?

Perhaps at the Christmas time we should check up on what we really feel—not what we agree to in public but the way we act, the ways in which we betray not only ourselves but the Child because our inner attitudes are ugly and disturbed.

Christmas candles make a lovely light across the country, and the scent of spruce and fir is spicy in the smallest home. The children sing the old carols and we hug to our hearts our boys and girls as we worship the Child in a manger. We pray silently that His Spirit will fill the world. But He cannot fulfill His promise through our children alone. We, the parents, must believe and act on our faith that His great joy was intended not just for ourselves or for a few, but for all people.

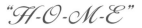

"H-O-M-E"

Dear Son Walter,

They'll be signing the formal surrender of Japan here in Tokyo Bay on September third. At last we'll have Peace on Earth again.

There's nothing adventurous or thrilling about war, son. I pray to God that we did a good job of making this the war to end all wars.

When you grow a little older you may think war to be a great adventure—take it from me it's the most horrible thing ever done by man.

I'll be home this Christmas and every Christmas from then on. Home (H-O-M-E) that's the place to stay. Take good care of Mama till I get there.

Love,
Your Dad

_____

*Chief Radioman
Walter G. Germann,
U.S. Navy, was in
Tokyo Bay for the
signing of the formal
surrender ending the
war. Shortly before
the ceremony, he put
it all in perspective in
a letter to his son.*

LEFT. After World War I, Warren G. Harding was elected president on a pledge of returning America to "normalcy." What could be more normal in this first post–World War II Christmas than a cornucopia of Christmas gifts in every stocking, including so many of those products unavailable during the conflict because of rationing? And whose stocking would it be more appropriate to fill with this Christmas cheer than the ones for the boys who have done so much for their country? This Macy's Christmas window gets right to the point with that sentiment. The store's theme for the display is "Now that it's over, let's make his Christmas merry wherever he is." ★ ★ ★

Text Sources

The editors are grateful for all the cooperation and permission granted for the text selections. Sources include the following:

I'll Be Home for Christmas lyrics reprinted by permission of Gannon & Kent, © 1943, renewed 1971.

1941

Page 8: Jim Wood, "Pearl Harbor Day in Beckley—A Sunday 40 Years Ago," Beckley, West Virginia: *Raleigh Register*, December 6, 1981.

Page 10: Website: http://home.earthlink.net/~bzleonard/betty6a.html.

Page 14: Franklin D. Roosevelt Library, Hyde Park, New York.

Page 15: *Cougar Scream,* published weekly aboard the USS *Washington,* December 13, 1941, available on website http://www.flash.net/~hfwright/13dec41.htm#4.

Page 17: Franklin D. Roosevelt Library, Hyde Park, New York.

Page 20: *The Washington Post,* December 25, 1941.

Page 20: Fred Edinger, "I'll Never Forget Pearl Harbor," *Homefront,* December 1944. Copyright © 1998 Homefront of the Slate Belt, Inc.

Page 21: Edward Vila, "Christmas and the Drums of War," Fleet Reserve Association, Alexandria, VA; website: http://www.fra.org/navalaffairs.

Page 24: Agnes P. Coleman, "Hawaii in 1941: A Joyous Christmas Despite the War," *Air Force Times,* December 21, 1998.

Page 27: *The New York Times,* December 25, 1941. Copyright © 1941 by the New York Times Co. Reprinted by permission.

Page 30: Judy Barrett Litoff and David C. Smith, eds., *Since You Went Away: World War II Letters from American Women on the Home Front.* New York, Oxford University Press, 1991, 7. Copyright © 1991 by Judy Barrett Litoff and David C. Smith. Used by permission of Oxford University Press, Inc.

1942

Page 35: *Journal of the Third Battalion,* December 25, 1942; Mississippi State University Historical Text Archive; available at website http://www.msstate.edu/Archives/History/USA/WWII/3bnlog.html.

Page 36: Franklin D. Roosevelt Library, Hyde Park, New York.

Page 36: *The Washington Post,* December 25, 1941.

Page 38: *The New York Times,* December 25, 1942.

Page 39: John H. Robinson, *A Reason to Live,* Memphis: Castle Books, 1988, 32.

Page 41: *The Washington Post,* December 21, 1942; reprinted in *The American War Mother,* Christmas issue, 1942, 7.

Page 43: *Poughkeepsie New Yorker,* November 29, 1942.

Page 44: Esther Carlson, "Christmas Wedding," *Good Housekeeping,* December 1993, 46. Used by permission of Esther Carlson.

Page 45: Joseph Desloge, *"My First Desert Christmas," Passport to Manhood: Adventures of a WWII Front Line Ambulance Driver with the British and the French Foreign Legion,* 1996; available on website http://www.icon-stl.net/~jdesloge/forward.html. Used by permission of Joseph Desloge.

Page 47: *Poughkeepsie New Yorker,* December 25, 1942; copyright, 1942, by United Feature Syndicate, Inc.

Page 48: Mary Ellin Barrett, *Irving Berlin: A Daughter's Memoir.* New York: Simon & Schuster, 1994, 208.

Page 50: Judy Barrett Litoff and David C. Smith, eds., *Since You Went Away: World War II Letters from American Women on the Home Front.* New York: Oxford University Press, 1991, 190. Copyright © 1991 by Judy Barrett Litoff and David C. Smith. Used by permission of Oxford University Press, Inc.

Page 51: Harry E. Maule, *A Book of War Letters.* New York: Random House, 1943, 141. Copyright © 1943 by Random House, Inc. Reprinted by permission of Random House, Inc.

Page 54: Harry E. Maule, *A Book of War Letters.* New York: Random House, 1943, 89. Copyright © 1943 by Random House, Inc. Reprinted by permission of Random House, Inc.

Page 60: Archie C. Rohrbaugh, "Chaplain's Message of the Month," *Homefront,* December 1942. Copyright © 1998 Homefront of the Slate Belt, Inc.

1943

Page 67: Hazel Hohn, "A World War II Christmas," *Christian Science Monitor,* December 13, 1995, 16. Used by permission of Hazel Hohn.

Page 69: Chaplain L. Clyde Carter, Jr., "Christmas Aboard a U.S. War Ship," USS New Orleans Reunion Association; website: http://purevictory.com/orleans/xmas.htm. Used by permission of Steven L. Carter.

Page 73: *Look,* December 15, 1943.

Page 76: "A Cook's Experiences in World War II"; website: http://www.kiva.net/~penguin/famhist/warstory.html; copyright © 1997 by John. A. Craton. Used by permission of John. A. Craton.

Page 78: Jeannette Stowe, "Peace on Christmas Day," 1943, Lincoln, Illinois; website: http://www.lincolnnet.net.

Page 79: Studs Terkel, *"The Good War": An Oral History of World War Two.* New York: Pantheon Books, 1984, 160.

Page 79: Robert F. Clarke, "Recollections," *American History,* February 1998, 68.

Page 82: Olive Bidwell Nowak, "A Busload of Strangers," *Good Housekeeping,* December 1993, 42.

Page 83: Philip Ardery, *Bomber Pilot: A Memoir of World War II.* Lexington: The University of Kentucky Press, 1978, 154. Copyright © 1996. Reprinted with the permission of The University Press of Kentucky.

Page 85: *Home Front and War Front in WWII: The Correspondence of Alfred de Grazia and Jill Oppenheim de Grazia,* December 21, 1943, with the permission of Metron Publications, copyright © 1998.

Page 87: H. H. Arnold to All Personnel of the Army Air Forces, December 25, 1943, Eaker Papers, Library of Congress.

Page 88: Charles E. Dibb, "Goodbye, Son," *The American War Mother,* December 1943, 6.

Page 92: Stanley A. Frankel, "Once Upon a Christmas . . ." *Frankel-y Speaking About World War II in the South Pacific;* website: http:///www.frankel-y.com/tape008.html. Used by permission of Stanley A. Frankel.

Page 96: Louisiana Tech Library; website: http://library.latech.edu/campruston/slide101.html; copyright © 1997 The Camp Ruston Foundation, Inc.

Page 96: *The New York Times,* December 25, 1943. Copyright © 1943 by the New York Times Co. Reprinted by permission.

Page 103: Tetsuzo Hirasaki to Clara Breed, December 29, 1943; website: http://www.lausd.k12.ca.us/janm/breed/12_29_43.t.html.

1944

Page 107: General Anthony McAuliffe to the Men of 101st Airborne Division, December 24, 1944, National Archives and Records Administration, RG 407.

Page 110: *Daughters of Pallas Athene,* Kansas City, Missouri: Women's Army Corps Veterans Association, 1983, 232. Used by permission of the Women's Army Corps Veterans Association.

Page 112: *Woman's Day,* December 1944.

Page 113: Erroll Laborde, "A Battlefield Christmas," *New Orleans Magazine,* December 1998, 4. Used by permission of Erroll Laborde.

Page 115: David Read, "Home by Christmas" *The Living Pulpit,* 1996; available at website http://www.pulpit.org; copyright © 1996 by The Living Pulpit, Inc.

Page 117: Adele Bernstein and Anne Hagner, "Jackson Street," *The Washington Post,* December 24, 1944.

Page 119: Sarah Winston, ed., *V-Mail: Letters of a World War II Combat Medic.* Chapel Hill, NC: Algonquin Books, 1985, 147. Copyright © 1985 by Sarah Winston. Reprinted by permission of Algonquin Books of Chapel Hill, a division of Workman Publishing.

Page 121: Heike Hasenauer, "A Desperate Gamble," *Soldiers Online;* website: http:www.dtic.mil/soldiers/dec94/p52.html./

Page 121: Charles Stockell memoir, Eisenhower Center, University of New Orleans; quoted in Stephen E. Ambrose, *Citizen Soldiers: The U.S. Army from the Normandy Beaches to the Bulge to the Surrender of Germany.* New York: Touchstone, 1997, 247.

Page 122: S. H. Kelly, "Christmas Birthdays and Snow: A Memoir of Winter in the Ardennes," *Pentagram,* December 19, 1997.

Page 126: Edward Andrusko, "Welcome Home and Merry Christmas," *Navy Times,* December 19, 1997.

Page 130: Bruce Egger and Lee Otts, *G-Company's War: Two Personal Accounts of the Campaign in Europe, 1944–1945.* Tuscaloosa: University of Alabama Press, 1992, 115; quoted in Stephen E. Ambrose, *Citizen Soldiers: The U.S. Army from the Normandy Beaches to the Bulge to the Surrender of Germany.* New York: Touchstone, 1997, 229.

Page 132: Richard M. Gordon, "Christmas Brings a Touch of Freedom," *The American Legion Magazine,* December 1998. Used by permission of Richard M. Gordon.

Page 134: Mary Hilbert, "Dead Son's Special Gift of Healing Love Helps Save Christmas," *Houston Chronicle,* December 20, 1998. Used by permission of Mary Hilbert.

Page 139: Franklin D. Roosevelt Library, Hyde Park, New York.

Page 142: USS Landing Craft Infantry National Association, "Holidays During Wartime"; website: http://www.usslci.com. Used by permission of Richard Bischoff.

Page 143: Carlo D'Este. *Patton: A Genius for War.* New York: HarperCollins Publishers, 1995, 686.

Page 144: Margaret Mass, "PFC Edward E. Benson," in the exhibit "The Sinking of the S.S. *Leopoldville*"; website: http://www.historychannel.com/exhibits/leopoldville/benson.html; copyright © 1998 A & E Television Networks.

Page 144: Bill Mauldin, *Stars and Stripes,* December 25, 1944; reprinted in *Up Front,* New York: W.W. Norton & Co., 1991, 227; originally published by Henry Holt & Company, Inc., 1945.

Page 145: A. Willard "Hap" Reese, "A Christmas Eve to Remember"; website: http://www.457thbombgroup.org. Used by permission of Willard Reese.

Page 152: Judy Barrett Litoff and David C. Smith, eds, *Since You Went Away: World War II Letters from American Women on the Home*

Front. New York: Oxford University Press, 1991, 108. Copyright © 1991 by Judy Barrett Litoff and David C. Smith. Used by permission of Oxford University Press.

Page 157: Jim Koerner, "Every day's a blessing," World War II Oral History; website: http://www.tankbooks.com/koerner.html. Used by permission of Aaron Elson.

Page 159: Lynn Grisard Fullman, "Army Surgeon at the Bulge," *Military History,* December 1996. Copyright © 1996 by Cowles History Group, Inc., d/b/a PRIMEDIA Enthusiast Publications, 741 Miller Drive, Suite D-2, Leesburg, VA 20175.

Page 159: *The New Yorker,* December 23, 1944, 503. Reprinted by permission, copyright © 1944 E. B. White. All rights reserved.

Page 161: Judy Litoff and David C. Smith, *Dear Boys: World War II Letters from a Woman Back Home.* Jackson: University of Mississippi Press, 1991, 216. Material is published with the permission of the University Press of Mississippi.

Page 162: Tony Valentino, "Imagination, Talent & Love," *The American Legion Magazine,* December 1998. Used by permission of Tony Valentino.

1945

Page 169: "VP-2 ATU-3-In Memorium-ATU-3 VP-2; website: http://erols.com/nfrankel/vp2mem_1216.html. Used by permission of Robert E. Woerner.

Page 172: Robert F. Williams, "A Salute to Number Two," *Trains,* June 1994, 41. Copyright © 1994 Kalmbach Publishing Company, reprinted with permission from the June 1994 issue of *Trains* magazine.

Page 177: Joyce Edwardson, "A Baby's Cry Was Serviceman's Delight," *West Central* (Minnesota) *Tribune.*

Page 178: Charles Newbury, "Thoughts of Home," *Los Angeles Times,* December 25, 1945; excerpts reprinted in Dana Parsons, "A Sentimental Holiday Letter Stands the Test of Time," *Los Angeles Times,* December 25, 1996.

Page 180: Mervyn Horder, "An International Christmas—Tokyo 1945," reprinted in *Contemporary Review,* December 1995, 281.

Page 186: Walter L. Cronkite, "Gen. Patton Joins Dead of His 3d Army in Hamm Cemetery," *Times Herald,* December 25, 1945. Copyright © 1945, *The Washington Post-Times Herald.* Reprinted with permission.

Page 190: Monte M. Poen, ed. *Letters Home by Harry Truman.* New York: G.P. Putnam's Sons, 1984, 200.

Page 191: Joseph H. Brennan, "Yule Merry for Crippled War Vets, Too," *Times-Herald,* December 25, 1945. Copyright © 1945, *The Washington Post–Times Herald.* Reprinted with permission.

Page 193: Sergeant A. Stotler to his sister, n.d., *Gettysburg* (Pennsylvania) *Times,* October 1945; website: http://www.gettysburg.edu.

Page 194: "Joy to All People," *Parents Magazine,* December 1945, 12. Copyright © 1945 Gruner + Jahr USA Publishing. Reprinted from *Parents Magazine* by permission.

Page 197: Walter Germann to his son, September 1, 1945, *World War II Personal Accounts: Pearl Harbor to V-J Day,* Washington, D.C.: National Archives and Records Administration, 1992, 374; copyright The Lyndon Baines Johnson Foundation, P.O. Box 1234, Austin Texas, 78701.

Photo Credits

Page 127   Library of Congress; Publishing Office Image Archive.
             National Archives and Record Service
Page 128   Library of Congress; Publishing Office Image Archive.
             National Archives and Record Service
Page 132   Library of Congress; Publishing Office Image Archive.
             National Archives and Record Service
Page 133   (Top and bottom): Library of Congress; Publishing Office
             Image Archive. National Archives and Record Service
Page 135   Library of Congress; Publishing Office Image Archive.
             National Archives and Record Service
Page 136   Library of Congress; Publishing Office Image Archive.
             National Archives and Record Service
Page 137   (Top and bottom): Library of Congress; Rare Book and
             Special Collections Division
Page 138   Library of Congress; Publishing Office Image Archive.
             National Archives and Record Service
Page 140   Library of Congress; Publishing Office Image Archive.
             National Archives and Record Service
Page 142   Library of Congress; Publishing Office Image Archive.
             National Archives and Record Service
Page 144   Bill Mauldin, *Stars and Stripes,* December 25,1944;
             reprinted in *UpFront,* New York: W. W. Norton & Co.,
             1991; originally published by Henry Holt & Company,
             Inc., 1945.
Page 145   Library of Congress; Publishing Office Image Archive.
             National Archives and Record Service
Page 146   Library of Congress; Publishing Office Image Archive.
             National Archives and Record Service
Page 148   Library of Congress; Publishing Office Image Archive.
             National Archives and Record Service
Page 150   Library of Congress; Publishing Office Image Archive.
             National Archives and Record Service
Page 151   Library of Congress; Manuscript Division
Page 153   Library of Congress; Publishing Office Image Archive.
             National Archives and Record Service
Page 154–155 Library of Congress; Publishing Office Image Archive.
             National Archives and Record Service
Page 156   (Top): Library of Congress; Publishing Office Image
             Archive. National Archives and Record Service
Page 156   (Bottom): Courtesy MacArthur Memorial, Norfolk, Va.
Page 158   Library of Congress; Publishing Office Image Archive.
             National Archives and Record Service
Page 160   Library of Congress; Publishing Office Image Archive.
             National Archives and Record Service